Year 5
Scottish Primary 6

50 Shared texts

Photocopiable texts for shared reading

- Fiction, non-fiction, poetry and drama
- Annotated versions
- Discussion prompts

Huw Thomas

Credits

Author
Huw Thomas

Illustrations
Angus Cameron

Series Consultants
Fiona Collins and
Alison Kelly

**Series
Designer**
Anna Oliwa

Editor
Clare Gallaher

Designer
Anna Oliwa

**Assistant
Editor**
Dulcie Booth

Text © 2003 Huw Thomas
© 2003 Scholastic Ltd

Designed using Adobe PageMaker

Published by Scholastic Ltd
Villiers House
Clarendon Avenue
Leamington Spa
Warwickshire CV32 5PR

www.scholastic.co.uk

Printed by Bell and Bain Ltd, Glasgow

2 3 4 5 6 7 8 9 0   4 5 6 7 8 9 0 1 2

British Library Cataloguing-in-Publication Data
A catalogue record for this book is available from
the British Library.

ISBN 0-439-98483-1

Contents

Ⓝ *Teacher's notes*   Ⓟ *Photocopiable*

Term 2

	N	P

Term 3

	N	P

 Teacher's notes   *Photocopiable*

Introduction

In *50 Shared texts* you will find a range of texts for use in shared reading. In recent years shared text work has become the focal point of daily literacy work, and the success of such shared work is clearly linked to the quality and choice of text. Better understanding of children's reading and writing development has led to the realisation that a greater range of text types, or genres, is needed to enrich children's literacy development. For the busy classroom teacher, seeking out such a range of quality texts can be too time-consuming, which is why appropriate texts have been provided in this book.

Shared reading

Shared reading is at the heart of the activities in this book and is a cornerstone of the National Literacy Strategy, which states that through shared reading children *begin to recognise important characteristics of a variety of written texts, often linked to style and voice.*

First developed in New Zealand by Don Holdaway, shared reading has been a significant literacy routine for children since the 1980s. Holdaway's research and pioneering work in schools brought the benefits of sharing enlarged texts or Big Books to teachers' attention. From his observations of very young children attending to bedtime stories on a one-to-one basis he realised that a similar intimacy with print could be offered through sharing an enlarged text with a group or class of children. He showed how engagement with Big Books can teach children about the characteristics of different text types, their organisation and distinguishing features, as well as the finer details of print. For example, depending on the teacher's focus, an enlarged recipe could be used at text level to model the way a piece of instructional writing is structured, at sentence level to look at the use of imperative verbs or at word level to focus on a particular phoneme. In relation to literature, the meaning

of a poem can be explored at text level, the poet's choice of verbs at sentence level and the rhyming pattern at word level. So, shared reading not only encourages the class to share the actual reading aloud of a text but also enables the teacher to discuss certain language features and support the children in both comprehending and responding to the text.

With younger children, shared reading involves following the text with a pointer to highlight key early concepts of print such as directionality and one-to-one correspondence. With such concepts securely in place, a rather different technique is needed for older children where the focus shifts more to understanding and responding to the text as well as discussing vocabulary and linguistic features. For all children, often the talk surrounding the reading is as important as the reading itself.

Finding the right quality texts for shared reading that will engage and interest the children, as well as meeting the many NLS objectives, can be a difficult task. Once a text is found, you need to identify salient features at word, sentence and text level.

Shared reading is also the springboard for shared writing, guided reading/writing and independent work. Both guided reading and writing provide opportunities for you to guide, support, model and comment on children's response to a text. Activities may involve reading aloud, role-play, performance or writing for a particular purpose. Independent activities may mirror these but need to be clearly structured to enable the children to work independently.

About this book

The texts in this book are organised term by term, following the NLS framework, so there are examples of fiction, poetry, plays and non-fiction.

For each text, both a blank and annotated version are provided. The former is for use with children and can either be enlarged or projected on an overhead projector; the latter is for teacher information and identifies the features of the text and links with NLS objectives.

Background

Background information is provided for each text. This will contextualise the extract, fill in any necessary details and give facts about its author as relevant. Information on themes, technical features or other related texts might also feature here.

Shared reading and discussing the text

This section offers guidance on ways of managing discussion around the text, as well as ways of organising the shared reading. Depending on the age of the children, and demands of the text, different strategies for working with the whole class on the text are given, as well as ways of triggering the children's responses. These include structured discussion suggestions, ideas for role-play, and performance techniques.

Activities

Building on the reading and discussion, this section suggests activities for both whole-class work and guided or independent group work. There are ideas for further textual analysis, sometimes involving shared writing. As in the previous section, talk is pivotal in developing the children's understanding.

Extension/further reading

Suggestions for taking activities into a broader context and ideas for linked reading are also provided, where appropriate. Reading may include books of the same genre, or texts that share the theme or the same author.

The texts

The choice of texts has been driven by the need to ensure that these are quality texts both in content and language. It is hoped that among the selection you will find a mixture of authors and texts, both familiar and new. Whole texts have been provided as far as possible so that children have the satisfaction of reading and appreciating a coherent and complete piece of writing.

Longer texts, such as novels, also need to feature in older children's reading, and sometimes more than one extract from the same carefully chosen novel has been included. Bearing in mind that children should experience as much of the novel as they can, it is recommended that you use the background notes to fill the children in on plot detail, and that you read the story to them or have copies, including a taped version, available for their own reading or listening. Other slots in the curriculum can be used for such reading: private reading, homework, independent group work or story time.

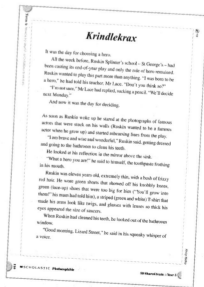

Range and objectives

Year 5 Term 1

Range	Text	NLS references
Novels by significant children's writers	**'Krindlekrax'** from *Krindlekrax* by Philip Ridley (Puffin Books)	S7, T1, T3, T15
	'Story openings' from *Snatchers* by Helen Cresswell (Hodder Children's Books), *Step by Wicked Step* by Anne Fine (Puffin Books) and *The Lottie Project* by Jacqueline Wilson (Corgi Yearling)	T1, T2, T9, T11
	'In the sewer: Krindlekrax' from *Krindlekrax* by Philip Ridley (Puffin Books)	T9, T14
	'The Gizmo' from *The Gizmo* by Paul Jennings (Puffin Books)	T2, T3, T9, T15
Stories by significant children's writers	**'Talk About Short'** from *Short! A Book of Very Short Stories* by Kevin Crossley-Holland (Oxford University Press)	W5, S6, S8, T1, T2, T9, T15, T18
Poems by significant children's writers	**'No-Speaks'** by Jackie Kay from *The Frog who dreamed she was an Opera Singer* (Bloomsbury Publishing)	T6, T7, T8
	'The New Poem' by Roger McGough from *Sky in the Pie* (Kestrel)	S1, S6, T6, T7, T8
Concrete poetry	**'Sky Day Dream' and 'Homeweb'** by Robert Froman from *Seeing Things* (Abelard-Schuman Ltd)	T6, T7, T8, T16
	'If the Earth' by Joe Miller	S6, T6, T8, T16
Playscripts	**'Martian Mama'** by Terry Halligan from *Funny Skits and Sketches* (Sterling Publishing Co, Inc)	T5, T18, T19, T20
	'Krindlekrax playscript' from the play *Krindlekrax* by Philip Ridley (Faber & Faber)	T3, T5, T18
	'Dear Brutus' from *Dear Brutus* by JM Barrie (Hodder & Stoughton)	W10, S5, T5, T9, T18
Recounts of events	**'A Little Bit From the Author'** by Paul Jennings from *Uncovered! Weird Weird stories* (Penguin Books Australia)	T4, T21, T24
	'Willy the Warthog' from *Death by Spaghetti: Bizarre, baffling and bonkers* by Paul Sussman (The Big Issue/Fourth Estate)	S4, S5, S7, S8, T21, T24
News reports	**'Unhappy ending for the newborn hippo'** (The Daily Mail)	S1, S3, T21, T24
Instructional texts: rules	**'Don't be a reject!'** from leaflet INS116R (DVLA)	S8, S9, T22, T25, T26
Instructional texts: showing how things are done	**'Your short story'** by Huw Thomas	S8, S9, T22, T25, T26
Instructions	**'Pick a Book'** from *Alan Snow's Whacky Guide to Tricks and Illusions* by Alan Snow and Louise Cook (Walker Books)	S8, S9, T22, T25, T26

Year 5 Term 2

Range	Text	NLS references
Myths from a range of cultures	**'The Creation'** from *Myths and Civilisations: Ancient Egyptians* by Sarah Quie (Franklin Watts)	W8, W10, T1, T11
	'The Hunting of Death' from *Golden Myths and Legends of the World* by Geraldine McCaughrean (Orion Children's Books)	T1, T11
	'Orpheus and Eurydice' from *The Orchard Book of Greek Myths* by Geraldine McCaughrean (Orchard Books)	S5, T1, T2, T11
Traditional stories from a range of cultures	**'Hare, Hippo and Elephant'** from *The Oxford Book of Children's Stories: South and North, East and West* edited by Michael Rosen (Walker Books)	S6, T1, T3, T11
Legends from a range of cultures	**'Till Owlyglass'** from *The Wicked Tricks of Till Owlyglass* by Michael Rosen (Walker Books)	S6, T1, T3, T11, T14
	'Sir Galahad' from *King Arthur and the Knights of the Round Table* by Marcia Williams (Walker Books)	S9, S10, T1
Fables from a range of cultures	**'Aesop's Fables'** from *Fables of Aesop* translated by SA Handford (Penguin Classics)	T1, T11
Narrative viewpoint	**'The Austere Academy'** from *A Series of Unfortunate Events: The Austere Academy* by Lemony Snicket (Egmont Books)	S3, T8
Longer classic poetry	**'Travel'** by Edna St Vincent Millay from *Collected Poems* by Edna St Vincent Millay (HarperCollins)	T7, T12
Longer classic poetry, including narrative poetry	**'An Elegy on the Death of a Mad Dog'** by Oliver Goldsmith from *Every Poem Tells a Story* edited by Raymond Wilson (Puffin Books)	S1, S8, T4, T6, T12
	'Journey of the Magi' by TS Eliot from *Selected Poems* (Faber & Faber)	T4, T6, T8, T10
	'Fairy Tale' by Miroslav Holub from *Selected Poems: Miroslav Holub* translated by Ian Milner and George Theiner (Penguin)	S4, S5, T4, T6, T10
Non-chronological reports	**'Sir Gawain'** from *The King Who Was and Will be* by Kevin Crossley-Holland (Orion Children's Books)	S8, T19, T22
	'The Sun' from *1001 Facts About Space* by Pam Beasant (Kingfisher Books)	W9, S4, T20, T22
	'The path that's not a promenade' from *The Guardian* (12 February 2000)	S5, S9, T20, T22
Explanations	**'The Stars'** from *1001 Facts About Space* by Pam Beasant (Kingfisher Books)	W9, T15, T16, T20
	'The game' from *Superguides: Football* by Gary Lineker (Dorling Kindersley)	W9, S5, S9, T15, T16

Year 5 Term 3

Range	Text	NLS references
Novels from a variety of cultures and traditions	**'Danger by Moonlight'** from *Danger by Moonlight* by Jamila Gavin (Egmont Books)	W12, T1, T2, T10
	'Black Angels' from *Black Angels* by Rita Murphy (Macmillan Children's Books)	T1, T2, T3, T8, T9
Stories from a variety of cultures and traditions	**'Travellers' Tales'** (extract 1) from *Travellers' Tales* by Anthony Masters (Blackie)	S4, S5, T1, T2, T3
	'Travellers' Tales' (extract 2) from *Travellers' Tales* by Anthony Masters (Blackie)	S4, T1, T2, T3
	'Anancy' from *Anancy-Spiderman* by James Berry (Walker Books)	W6, T1, T6
Poems from a variety of cultures and traditions	**'The Three Magi'** from *Spoiling Cannibals' Fun: Polish Poetry of the Last Two Decades of Communist Rule* by Stanislaw Baranczak (Northwestern University Press)	S6, T1, T5, T10
	'Morning' by Dionne Brand from *Can I Buy a Slice of Sky?* edited by Grace Nichols (Hodder)	S3, S4, S6, T1
	'Tao Te Ching' from *Tao Te Ching* of Lao Tzu, translated by Gia-Fu Feng and Jane English (Ashgate Publishing)	T1, T6, T9
Choral and performance poetry	**'Picnic Poem'** from *Creaking Down the Corridor* by David Harmer and Paul Cookson (BBC Verse Universe)	T4, T11
	'Stopping by Woods on a Snowy Evening' from *The Poetry of Robert Frost* (Henry Holt & Co)	T4, T6
Persuasive writing to put or argue a point of view: letters	**'Sport on TV'** letter from the *Radio Times* (27 April to 3 May 2002)	T12, T14, T15, T17, T19
	'Age of majority is not a minor matter' letter from the *Times Educational Supplement* (3 May 2002)	T12, T14, T15, T19
Persuasive writing to put or argue a point of view: commentaries	**'edleader'** from *Junior Education* (Scholastic, June 2002)	S4, S6, T13, T14, T15
Dictionaries	**'Dictionary definitions'**: extract 1 from *The Ginn School Dictionary* by George Hunt (Heinemann Rigby); extract 2 from *Chambers' Handy Dictionary* (Chambers Harrap); extract 3 from *Chambers' Twentieth Century Dictionary* (Chambers Harrap)	W11, W12, S2, T14
Thesauruses	**'Thesaurus entries'**: extract 1 from *The Oxford Children's Thesaurus* (Oxford University Press); extract 2 from *Better Words: A First Thesaurus* by C Windridge (Schofield & Sims)	W5, W6, W9, W11, S2

Krindlekrax

by Philip Ridley

Background

The opening of the contemporary classic, *Krindlekrax,* introduces children to the character who will not only manage to be the hero of the story but also challenge what the word *hero* means. Much of the story hinges on Ruskin being portrayed as the opposite of the traditional hero, yet he manages to save his street from the menacing lizard, Krindlekrax.

Shared reading and discussing the text

● Read the opening line to the children and ask them to tell you any questions they have about the sentence. They may say, *Which hero? Who will choose a hero? Why is one needed?* Then share the first full paragraph with them. Point out the way in which an opening line hooks the reader, appealing to our inquisitiveness.

● Ask the children what they think of when they hear the word *hero*. To stimulate this it might be worth listing some of the features of well-known heroic figures, such as Superman or Hercules. List some of their responses on the board and keep these to one side.

● Now read the opening of the text as far as *He looked at his reflection in the mirror above the sink*. Try creating a shared text that would describe what the children think a hero would see when he looked at himself in a mirror – perhaps *He looked at…* or *He admired his…* and ask them to think of traditional qualities.

● Read Mr Lace's response to Ruskin. Ask the children to think of five different ways in which the teacher could have responded to Ruskin's question. Why do they think the teacher, Mr Lace, responded in the way he did? There will be a variety of possible reasons offered to do with everyone being given a chance, and so on.

● Annotate the way in which speech is demarcated in the text – the use of speech marks, commas and one exclamation mark. Look at the different verbs used for *said* in the passage. Point out the use of alternate lines for each speaker.

● Read the rest of the passage. Discuss the various ways in which a character can be presented. There is Ruskin's speech in which he confidently puts himself forward as the hero. This is at odds with his appearance. Circle the adjectives (for example *extremely thin, knobbly*) that build up our image of him. Locate and mark his actions – looking at himself, approaching his teacher and whispering to his street. These all give an insight into his character. At the end of the text, do we still think of Ruskin as a heroic figure? If not, point out features in this description that have changed our initial assumption. Will he be the hero?

● Ask the children to think of other stories in which an unlikely character turns out to be the hero or heroine. This is a common feature of children's fiction and traditional tales. Think of Peter defeating the wolf, foolish Jack beating the giant and ragged Cinderella going to the ball. Ask the children to think of a particular example and how the character was initially perceived. What did he or she do to change this perception?

Activities

● Ask the children to write two different story openings, choosing the same location for each. In one they must present what they think a reader would expect from a straightforward heroine or hero; in the other they must introduce a character who does not correspond to expectation.

● Can the children plan a story in which both the above characters will feature? How can they make the less conventional hero or heroine be the one the reader eventually elevates to this position?

● Children can write a short conversation between Ruskin and Mr Lace in the playground that morning. How would Mr Lace sensitively handle Ruskin's keenness to play the hero?

Extension/further reading

Two other Ridley stories, *ZinderZunder* and *Kaspar in the Glitter* (both Puffin Books), present similar openings in which we are introduced to unheroic characters. In both these, the characters eventually show their heroic qualities.

questions
raised by
opening line

followed by
some
explanation

speech marks
and comma

a new line for
a new speaker

characters
presented
through:

their
environment

their speech

their
appearance

their actions

verbs for speech

adjectives help
us visualise the
character

how he looks
contrasts with
the part he
wants to play

problem
presented: can
Ruskin be the
hero?

is this the sound
of a hero?

Krindlekrax

It was the day for choosing a hero.

All the week before, Ruskin Splinter's school – St George's – had been casting its end-of-year play and only the role of hero remained. Ruskin wanted to play this part more than anything. "I was born to be a hero," he had told his teacher, Mr Lace. "Don't you think so?"

"I'm not sure," Mr Lace had replied, sucking a pencil. "We'll decide next Monday."

And now it was the day for deciding.

As soon as Ruskin woke up he stared at the photographs of famous actors that were stuck on his walls (Ruskin wanted to be a famous actor when he grew up) and started rehearsing lines from the play.

"I am brave and wise and wonderful," Ruskin said, getting dressed and going to the bathroom to clean his teeth.

He looked at his reflection in the mirror above the sink.

"What a hero you are!" he said to himself, the toothpaste frothing in his mouth.

Ruskin was eleven years old, extremely thin, with a bush of frizzy red hair. He wore green shorts that showed off his knobbly knees, green (lace-up) shoes that were too big for him ("You'll grow into them!" his mum had told him), a striped (green and white) T-shirt that made his arms look like twigs, and glasses with lenses so thick his eyes appeared the size of saucers.

When Ruskin had cleaned his teeth, he looked out of the bathroom window.

"Good morning, Lizard Street," he said in his squeaky whisper of a voice.

Story openings

by Helen Cresswell, Anne Fine and Jacqueline Wilson

Extracts 1, 2 and 3

P 111

Background

These three story openings – each from novels by significant children's authors – launch us into the stories in different ways. Among the three openings there is a narrator opening a story, characters being plunged into a scary setting, and a character anticipating a potential conflict in the future. All address the reader in a way that immediately sets the tone.

Shared reading and discussing the text

● Ask the children to read each of the openings and think about the sorts of things that may happen in each story. Where will the characters go and what will they do? Discuss what settings and situations may be presented.

● Encourage the children to list the differences between the opening sentences – a narrator with an authorial voice; a sentence which reveals the setting; and a school child stating her clear intentions and opinion. What questions does each one raise?

● Focus on the language used in each extract. Draw three columns on the board and ask the children to pick out five words in each opening that seem quite particular to that specific text. One way of choosing these is to read the text, then conceal it, asking children which words they still remember – words like *haunted* and *simple-pimple*, for example. Once the three columns are completed, ask the children to contrast the type of language – from the informal to the dramatic. Having looked at this, approach each paragraph with the question *What sort of story is this going to be?*

● Re-read the opening of *Step by Wicked Step*. Circle the features that give a sense of mystery and scariness – the wild night (ask *How can a night be wild?*), the dramatic 'There!', 'Where?' as they struggle to see the house in the darkness. Encourage the children to draw on their knowledge of other stories which have the same traditional scary features.

● Ask the children what they consider strange about the opening to *Snatchers*. How is it different from other story openings they have

read? What is the effect of the opening command to *Listen…*? Note the informal and chatty style that the author uses. Work through the passage, pointing to each sentence and encouraging the children to think about questions that may arise in the reader's mind in response to the text.

● The opening to *Krindlekrax* (see page 10) involves an initial encounter with a character. What do we learn about Charlie (the narrator of extract 3) and Ruskin (in *Krindlekrax*) from the openings? In a shared session, make notes about the characters, including the children's own original ideas.

Activities

● Provide the children with five novels selected from the school library and ask them to review the opening paragraphs. Which ones are most like the three here or the one from *Krindlekrax*? Can they find another example of a narrator retelling a story, one that focuses on the setting, or a character looking ahead to what might happen in the future?

● Working in small groups, the children can take two of the opening paragraphs and create a list of questions that they have about the story that will follow each opening.

● Ask the children to write one opening paragraph that matches the style of one of the three texts. Allow them to choose the subject matter.

● Basing their opinions on the opening paragraphs, can the children rate which stories they would want to read, putting them in order of preference? They should note down what drew them into the story as well as anything they found off-putting.

Extension/further reading

Snatchers, *Step by Wicked Step* and *The Lottie Project* all live up to their excellent opening paragraphs. Children could compare these openings with others in stories by the same writers. They could also revisit stories they have read and look at their opening paragraphs.

5: 1: T1: to analyse the features of a good opening and compare a number of story openings

5: 1: T2: to compare the structure of different stories, to discover how they differ in pace, build-up, sequence, complication and resolution

Story openings

title to grab the reader

narrator's voice

chatty, confidential style

SNATCHERS

BEFORE YOU BEGIN…

Listen, I have a story to tell. It's mad and sad in parts and beautiful as well. Most stories have a time and a place. They happen because a particular person was in a particular place at a particular time. Think about it. If Wendy Darling had not lived in a certain tall house in a certain street in London, we should never have known the story of Peter Pan.

The particular person in this story is called Ellie. But I don't know when it happened, or where.

no clues given about the setting

ambiguity raises questions in the reader's mind

opening that creates the setting

the weather has made the night turn wild

dramatic effect of dialogue

STEP BY WICKED STEP

Even before they reached the haunted house, the night had turned wild. The face of the minibus driver flickered from blue to white under the lightning. Each peal of thunder made the map in Mr Plumley's hand shiver. And the five leftover pupils from Stagfire School peered anxiously through the rain-spattered windows into the storm and the black night.

"There!"

"Where?"

"Over there. See? Up that overgrown driveway."

feelings evoked by thoughts of other stories

pupils are 'leftovers' – they are the only ones remaining

conventional elements of a scary setting

title gives the setting

how could someone know this? teacher told her? she planned it?

opening launches straight into the situation

THE LOTTIE PROJECT

SCHOOL

I knew exactly who I was going to sit next to in class. Easy-peasy, simple-pimple. It was going to be Angela, with Lisa sitting at the nearest table to us. I'm never quite sure if I like Lisa or Angela best, so it's only fair to take turns.

Jo said what if Angela and Lisa want to sit together with *you* behind or in front or at the side.

informal style

presents characters through their words and thoughts

each opening makes the reader think about what sort of story it is going to be

5: 1: T9: to develop an active attitude towards reading: seeking answers, anticipating events, empathising with characters and imagining events that are described

5: 1: T11: to experiment with alternative ways of opening a story using, e.g. description, action, or dialogue

In the sewer: Krindlekrax

by Philip Ridley

Background

Philip Ridley often uses short chapters – some as short as a word – to build up the pace in his stories. This extract is from a short chapter from *Krindlekrax* and is a classic example of the building up of suspense. Following the death of his dear friend Corky, a retired sewer worker who told Ruskin about the creature that lives under the street, Ruskin decides to rid the people of Lizard Street of Krindlekrax. He stays up all night, aiming to catch the monster. His plans take a turn for the worst when he drops Corky's treasured walking stick down into the sewer and has to descend the ladder from the drain cover to retrieve it. We have reached the climax of the book and this will be the point at which he encounters the monster.

Shared reading and discussing the text

● Before reading the text, give the children some background to this stage in the story and ask them to list things that could happen when Ruskin enters the sewer. This passage thrives on the reader's sense that something will happen soon, and it is structured to delay the encounter with the rats and then with the monster.

● Share the 'mapping' of this part of the story with the children. Ask them to find ups and downs in the passage, ups being points where things look up for Ruskin (such as when he first sees the stick or realises the beauty of the sewers), downs being moments like the coldness of the sewer, or the stick moving away from him. Put these events in order of their occurrence, writing them across the board and marking each one with an up or down arrow.

● Children should begin to see the way in which the two extremes are interspersed – a positive moment such as the sighting of the stick is snatched away by a negative, as the stick is carried off by the current. Ask the children how they think this affects the reader. Point out that it maintains the tension and keeps us reading.

● Much of the suspense created by the text lies in the setting. We see everything through Ruskin's torchlight, which makes his surroundings even more mysterious and unknown. Pick out parts of the text that develop the reader's understanding of what the sewer is like, and help us to imagine how Ruskin's senses are affected – the *echoing sounds that made his eardrums ring,* for example. The sewer is *cold* and the green slime *sparkled like emeralds*. The water is *satin smooth*. Can the children see how the different descriptions and use of metaphor reflect Ruskin's changing feelings about the sewer?

● Review the first Krindlekrax extract (see page 10) and remind the children of the discussions about whether Ruskin had the making of a hero. How is he squaring up after this extract? Is he heroic? What makes the difference between our appraisal of him now and in the earlier passage?

Activities

● Ask the children to imagine Ruskin took a tape recorder down into the sewer with him. Can they script the thoughts he might have spoken into the recorder, to form a monologue?

● Map out the journey through the sewer in diagrammatic form on a large sheet of paper, drawing a drain cover, ladder, ledge and the rats. On this map ask the children to write what they think Ruskin would be thinking, seeing and hearing at different stages along his journey. Use the map to explore the different verbs used by the author: *stretched, reached, jumped, flickered, sparkled* and so on. Can the children point out where these actions take place on the map?

Extension/further reading

From this point onwards, the story takes an unexpected turn, creating an unusual encounter with the monster. If you have access to a copy of the book it is well worth reading the entire story.

Philip Ridley's *Dakota of the White Flats* (Puffin Books) provides another example of a heroic journey undertaken through an urban setting.

5: 1: T9: to develop an active attitude towards reading: seeking answers, anticipating events, empathising with characters and imagining events that are described

5: 1: T14: to map out texts showing development and structure, e.g. its high and low points, the links between sections, paragraphs, chapters

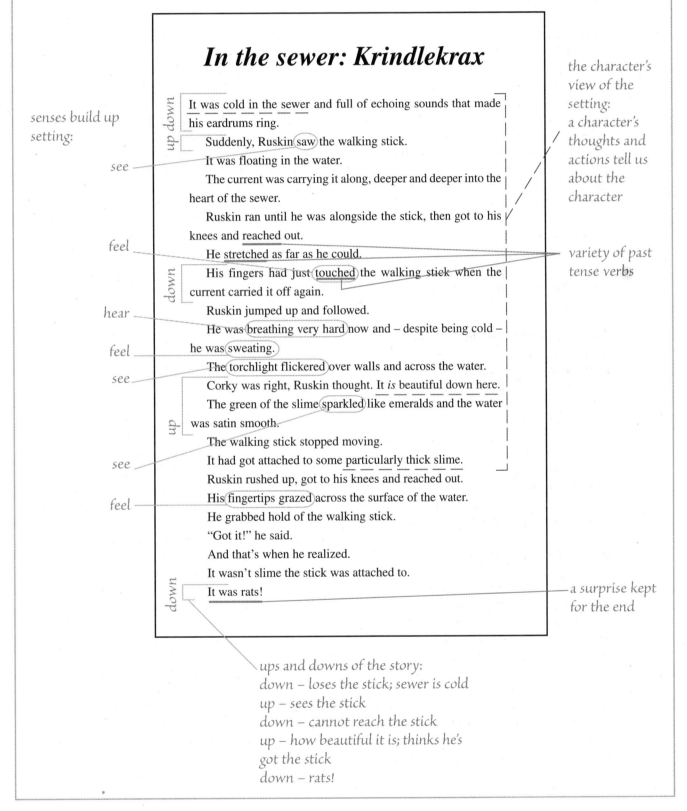

In the sewer: Krindlekrax

senses build up setting:

up down

see

It was cold in the sewer and full of echoing sounds that made his eardrums ring.

Suddenly, Ruskin saw the walking stick.

It was floating in the water.

The current was carrying it along, deeper and deeper into the heart of the sewer.

Ruskin ran until he was alongside the stick, then got to his knees and reached out.

feel

He stretched as far as he could.

down

His fingers had just touched the walking stick when the current carried it off again.

hear

Ruskin jumped up and followed.

He was breathing very hard now and – despite being cold – he was sweating.

feel

see

The torchlight flickered over walls and across the water.

Corky was right, Ruskin thought. It *is* beautiful down here.

up

The green of the slime sparkled like emeralds and the water was satin smooth.

The walking stick stopped moving.

It had got attached to some particularly thick slime.

see

Ruskin rushed up, got to his knees and reached out.

feel

His fingertips grazed across the surface of the water.

He grabbed hold of the walking stick.

"Got it!" he said.

And that's when he realized.

It wasn't slime the stick was attached to.

down

It was rats!

the character's view of the setting:
a character's thoughts and actions tell us about the character

variety of past tense verbs

a surprise kept for the end

ups and downs of the story:
down – loses the stick; sewer is cold
up – sees the stick
down – cannot reach the stick
up – how beautiful it is; thinks he's got the stick
down – rats!

The Gizmo

by Paul Jennings

Background

The gizmo is a gadget that features in a series of short books by the Australian writer, Paul Jennings. It always punishes the central character in some way – in this story it has a grip upon Stephen, the narrator. He has stolen it from a market stall and, as the story progresses, he changes clothes with any person he looks at. In this extract he has lost his own clothes to a tramp and, when the gizmo beeps, trades those in for a bride's wedding dress. After this, he ends up in a pink bikini and then naked.

Shared reading and discussing the text

● This is one text you might consider not reading in full on its first airing. Explain the dilemma facing the narrator – he is plagued by a gizmo that will swap his clothes with another person's whenever it hums and then beeps. Read as far as the words *a long white dress* and ask the children what they think could happen next. Read on as far as the gizmo's hum. Ask them to explain why Stephen shouts, *'No...'*

● Read through the scene to gather some of the ways in which the character of Stephen is presented. Ask the children to ascertain from the text the following: what he looks like, the thoughts he has, the words that show us what he is thinking or feeling, his thoughts and opinions regarding other characters and the things he does. These clues give us an insight into how the character is coping with the situation he has found himself in. Ask the children to say what they have learned about Stephen from their reading of this passage.

● Look through the passage, marking out the words and phrases that reveal the character of the bride. Underline the pointers to her appearance, what others think of her and the things she does.

● The scene is a wedding. Ask the children to think of the sort of behaviour people adopt in such formal situations. Return to an exploration of how Stephen is affected by the other characters – note his comments about the bride and the groom, particularly the *dressed to kill* comment. Bring these observations to bear on the last four sentences. How do these thoughts contribute to the fun we have reading about the change brought about by the gizmo?

● Ask the children why they think a scene like this works so well. What makes it gripping? The reader gains some idea of how the scene will end as the characters make eye contact. How is the excitement for the reader built up?

Activities

● Ask the children to devise their own ideas for embarrassing clothes changes that could take place within this story. They might want to consider changes which involve characters in uniforms, fancy dress costumes, or clothes that are too big or too small for them.

● Ask the children to consider their own gizmo dilemmas. Can they plan a storyline in which a gadget beeps and produces repeated changes?

● Using ideas produced in the above activities, the children could devise in detail their own scene in which their gizmo beeps at the end. As with this extract, in which the reader gradually realises what is coming, they need to let their scene build up to the final hum and beep. They should think about their central character, how he or she responds to other characters and the way this is integrated into the ending.

Extension/further reading

The other *Gizmo* stories, including *The Gizmo Again* and *Sink the Gizmo* (all Puffin Books), present further dilemmas as the gadget beeps. In these texts, the changes are similarly charted – clothes being swapped, people becoming dogs... each change taking place in a situation devised to maximise embarrassment.

5: 1: T2: to compare the structure of different stories, to discover how they differ in pace, build-up, sequence, complication and resolution

5: 1: T3: to investigate how characters are presented, referring to the text:
- through dialogue, action and description
- how the reader responds to them (as victims, heroes, etc.)
- through examining their relationships with other characters

The Gizmo

character presented:

The tramp disappears around a corner. By the time I turn it he is nowhere to be seen. The street is full of people who are coming out of a church. It is a wedding and all the people are dressed in their best clothes and throwing confetti.

gives a sense of how people behave at weddings

what the character says

"He is hiding," I say to myself. "The tramp is hiding in the crowd." I start to push through the people, trying to find the tramp.

what the character does

"Go away," sniffs a lady as I push past her legs. "Dreadful boy. Smelly. Awful. How dare you dress like that at a wedding. Go away."

how others respond to the character

I pretend not to hear. I have to get my clothes back or Dad will kill me. Suddenly I find myself staring at the bride. She is beautiful. Lovely. Nearly as good as my girlfriend Kate. She wears a veil in her hair. And flowers. And a long white dress.

what the character thinks

clue to what will happen later

Two little kids in purple are holding a long train out at the back. Her new husband is standing next to her, all dressed up to kill. I recognise him. He is the coach of our local football team. At the back is the preacher. His head nearly falls off when he sees me and my outfit.

how the character looks

The bride looks at me. And I look at her. She is shocked to see a boy dressed like a tramp.

Suddenly there is a hum. It is coming from my pocket. "No, no, please no," I scream. The crowd are all looking at me. Everyone falls silent. The gizmo beeps.

makes the reader wonder what is going to happen

build-up of tension culminates in climax

And the bride is dressed like a tramp.

And I am dressed like a bride.

She opens her mouth and screams in horror. I open my mouth and scream in horror.

repetition

5: 1: T9: to develop an active attitude towards reading: seeking answers, anticipating events, empathising with characters and imagining events that are described

5: 1: T15: to write new scenes or characters into a story, in the manner of the writer, maintaining consistency of character and style, using paragraphs to organise and develop detail

Talk About Short by Kevin Crossley-Holland

Background

It's short, but contains all you could look for in a story. This text comes from the unique collection, *Short!* by Kevin Crossley-Holland, a book of original or retold stories, all of which have the common feature of being less than two sides of a page in length. A number of the stories are urban myths or creepy tales –of which this is a prime example. This text shows just how short a story can be. Yet within it we have a character, a setting, a situation that gets more complicated, unanswered questions, a twist in the tail and a response from the reader.

Shared reading and discussing the text

● Read the story with the children and ask them for their immediate responses. They will point to the length and might raise questions about what happened. Discuss with them the question *What makes a story?*, listing their responses on the board. Having collated the list, evaluate this text to see whether or not it can be classed as a story.

● Look at the character and setting of the story. Who could this character be and where could he be? Interesting discussion can be developed on why readers tend to assume he is inside rather than outside. Where would a character need to grope around for matches? Finally, consider how they think this man must be feeling at the end of the story. The usual assumption is 'scared' or 'shocked' –but what if he was distraught to be alone? Could those last seven words be a message of support?

● Even after considering the above, the story leaves a lot unanswered. Ask the children to split into two groups. Explain that one half is going to raise a question they have about the tale and the other half is going to provide an answer;

then the question and answer roles will be reversed. They won't find answers in the text but they can share in generating their own.

● This story provides a good example of the use of the semi-colon, separating two clear and distinct clauses while not totally splitting them apart. It's like a full stop that says, 'But this sentence isn't over yet'. It is well placed here as it stands before the twist in the tale. We've been told 'he' is alone –well, is he?

● Beginning with the word *matches*, collect together other words with soft endings that use *es* to form their plural (*dish, fox, wish, stitch*) and ask the children to write the plurals for these nouns.

Activities

● The story is 22 words long. Ask the children to attempt to write a complete story within 30 words. They could vary the genre, attempting a love story or a comic tale, for example. Given the brevity of the task, ask the children to try various verbs to get precisely the right one for the atmosphere of their story.

● Produce a radio play that begins with the noise of that match being struck. Who else is in this dark setting and what do the two characters say to each other?

● Ask the children to produce a soundtrack to accompany a retelling of the tale, using a variety of percussion instruments. How will they convey the loneliness or the darkness? How will they end their piece?

Extension/further reading

Look through tabloid newspapers to find news reports condensed to five lines or less. What questions do readers still have about these stories?

5: 1: T1: to analyse the features of a good opening and compare a number of story openings

5: 1: T2: to compare the structure of different stories, to discover how they differ in pace, build-up, sequence, complication and resolution

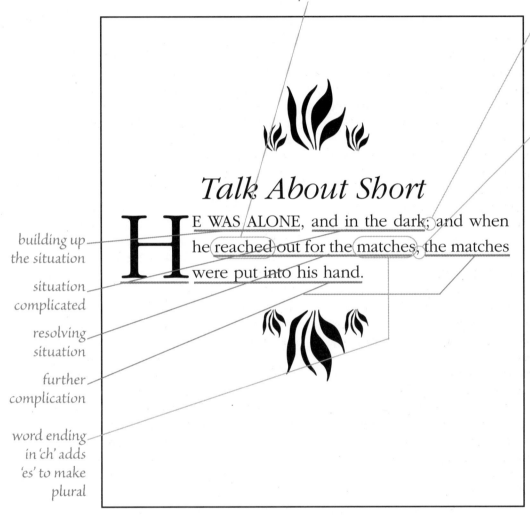

use of the right verb – helps the reader to imagine the scene, and has a particular effect

use of semi-colon to divide clauses

use of comma

Talk About Short

HE WAS ALONE, and in the dark; and when he reached out for the matches, the matches were put into his hand.

building up the situation

situation complicated

resolving situation

further complication

word ending in 'ch' adds 'es' to make plural

poses questions: who is he? where is he? why is he alone? who hands the matches to him? how does the reader respond to this character? what would it feel like to be this man?

5: 1: T9: to develop an active attitude towards reading: seeking answers, anticipating events, empathising with characters and imagining events that are described

5: 1: T15: to write new scenes or characters into a story, in the manner of the writer, maintaining consistency of character and style, using paragraphs to organise and develop detail

5: 1: T18: write own playscript, applying conventions learned from reading; include production notes

5: 1: S6: to understand the need for punctuation as an aid to the reader, e.g. commas to mark grammatical boundaries; a colon to signal, e.g. a list

5: 1: S8: to revise and extend work on verbs

5: 1: W5: to investigate, collect and classify spelling patterns in pluralisation, construct rules for regular spellings, e.g. add -s to most words; add -es to most words ending in -s, -sh, -ch

No-Speaks

by Jackie Kay

Background

This text, from Jackie Kay's collection *The Frog who dreamed she was an Opera Singer*, is a mysterious poem about a child who does not speak. The details we gather are that she just stopped speaking, not through any trauma but as a personal decision. 'No-Speaks' tells us she *clocked it was a waste of time* and so stopped talking.

The poem's power lies in the fact that a girl who never speaks is, in these lines, opening up and talking about her silence. Jackie Kay is a poet who often deals with the personal feelings and inner voices of people, presenting their fears, complaints and losses in poetic form.

Shared reading and discussing the text

● Ask the children to read the poem through once, quietly, to themselves. Explain that as they do this they will understand some of the lines clearly, while others will puzzle them. Once they have completed a silent skimming of the text, encourage them to offer some facts about *the child* whose voice we are hearing (for example, *She hasn't spoken for three years*).

● The first two lines hook the reader immediately. Why would someone stop speaking? Discuss with the children their insights into this – they may even know a child who gets by without using verbal communication, either because they can't or don't use the language of those around them. What sorts of difficulties would this present? Develop this into a discussion about times when children can recall not wanting to speak, being too embarrassed to speak or wishing things would be quieter. What about the notion of speaking being a waste of time and that it is better to be the silent watcher?

● Looking at the wordplay in the poem, circle all the nouns. Then ask the children to identify what each of the nouns actually does (for example, the snow melts, the tongue is held). There are some interesting actions performed by nouns in the poem. One of the main verbs performed by No-Speaks is to watch. Find all the

instances of this. What does she actually watch?

● Look closer at the description of the trees and the snow. Two powerful ideas in this poem are the silence and the passing of time. Point out the way in which the trees are personified (they *grow big beards*, they have *fuzzy hair* and *get alopecia*). How does likening the trees changing to the ageing of a person convey the passage of time?

● The poem has an irregular rhyme scheme. Can the children pick out words that rhyme (and half-rhymes)? How does the rhyming of lines affect the rhythm of the poem when the children read it aloud? Does it make them say lines quickly or slowly? Are certain bits harder to say? Do certain parts flow with rhyming lines? This is a clear example of form affecting meaning. Point out the way in which rhyme can help define different sections of the poem (for example, the lines ending in *time* and *rhyme* create a new section, separate from the previous lines ending in *Speaks*, *weeks* and *speech*).

● *If two people tell the same lie at the same time, one will die before the year is over.* Ask the children to think of other examples of playground folklore to do with 'jinxing' and two people speaking at the same time. Point out the significance of the brackets around this text, which makes it seem like an afterthought.

Activities

● Ask the children to write a playscript in which No-Speaks is present in a room where two or more people are talking. Explain that we will be able to hear her thoughts, as in a play or film, and these should take the form of asides to the audience. Less able children could write the thoughts No-Speaks has in a particular situation.

● Ask the children to write a letter to No-Speaks, responding to what she has said in the poem. They will need to consider whether they are going to persuade her to break her silence. They will also want to ask her questions and comment on her decision not to speak, trying to work out the reasoning behind it.

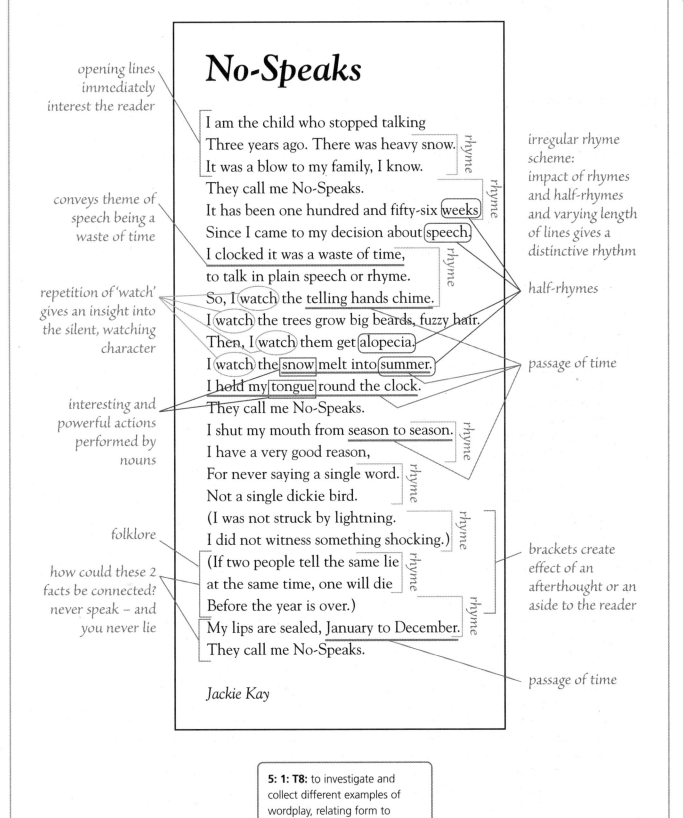

5: 1: T6: to read a number of poems by significant poets and identify what is distinctive about the style or content of their poems

5: 1: T7: to analyse and compare poetic style, use of forms and the themes of significant poets; to respond to shades of meaning; to explain and justify personal tastes; to consider the impact of full rhymes, half rhymes, internal rhymes and other sound patterns

opening lines immediately interest the reader

No-Speaks

I am the child who stopped talking
Three years ago. There was heavy snow.
It was a blow to my family, I know.
They call me No-Speaks.
It has been one hundred and fifty-six weeks
Since I came to my decision about speech.
I clocked it was a waste of time,
to talk in plain speech or rhyme.
So, I watch the telling hands chime.
I watch the trees grow big beards, fuzzy hair.
Then, I watch them get alopecia.
I watch the snow melt into summer.
I hold my tongue round the clock.
They call me No-Speaks.
I shut my mouth from season to season.
I have a very good reason,
For never saying a single word.
Not a single dickie bird.
(I was not struck by lightning.
I did not witness something shocking.)
(If two people tell the same lie
at the same time, one will die
Before the year is over.)
My lips are sealed, January to December.
They call me No-Speaks.

Jackie Kay

conveys theme of speech being a waste of time

repetition of 'watch' gives an insight into the silent, watching character

interesting and powerful actions performed by nouns

folklore

how could these 2 facts be connected? never speak – and you never lie

irregular rhyme scheme: impact of rhymes and half-rhymes and varying length of lines gives a distinctive rhythm

rhyme

half-rhymes

passage of time

brackets create effect of an afterthought or an aside to the reader

passage of time

5: 1: T8: to investigate and collect different examples of wordplay, relating form to meaning

The New Poem

by Roger McGough

Background

One of the 'Mersey Sound' poets of the Sixties, Roger McGough has popularised poems for all ages. He is a well-known performer of his own work and presents poetry on television, stage and radio.

This poem is an example of his tendency to turn wordplay into a well-developed poem.

Shared reading and discussing the text

● Read through the poem once and ask the children if they can explain why it has this particular title. What happens to the 18 words as the stanzas progress? They may take time to realise that the same 18 words reappear each time, but they should perceive the last stanza as being more accessible than the previous two. Return to the beginning and ask the children to look for the way in which the poet plays with the words throughout the poem.

● Can the children re-read the first stanza as a new reader encountering the poem for the first time? How would they make sense of the two sentences? What could be meant by the term *New words* and how could they be on their way to *Where they have not yet got*?

● Moving on to the second stanza, can the children import some sense into the statement and question? Here there is the novel idea of words that have not got used to their current situation. Ask the children if they can appreciate the notion of these words not being settled and contented. Re-reading the first two stanzas of the poem, ask the children to pick out lines and phrases that do, and do not, make sense. Can they find any other way of using some of the 18 words to make a new statement or question (for example, *The poem is new words not used*)? You could allow them to use the same word twice (*The words are not used to being used*).

● Explore the theme of the poem. In what ways can the writing of a poem be like the moving around of words that are not yet where they are used to being? Point out the fact that producing poetry often involves agonising over the arrangement of a small number of words to create effective lines.

Activities

● Ask the children to write a sentence which contains 15 to 18 words. They should then write the sentence on a strip of card and cut out the individual words. Can they devise a new sentence out of the old words? Encourage them to use as many of the words as they can. They may find interesting rearrangements that can be made if they change specific words.

● Create a strip of 18 words, using the same ones from the poem. Cut out the words and challenge the children to recreate any of the three stanzas without looking at the original text.

● Can the children think of other things they could write about words, or devise situations in which certain words are the central characters? For example, the five aside team who asked *Have goal we scored a?*, then *Have we scored a goal?*, until their words were rearranged to become *We have scored a goal*. In McGough's poem the words find their way into their correct places. Ask the children to devise a short piece of writing that presents a story about a set of words, or plays with the idea of certain words working together. Could a group of words work together to make an instruction or a greeting?

Extension/further reading

This poem is taken from McGough's collection *Sky in the Pie*. It contains a number of other examples of wordplay, such as 'The Writer of this Poem' and 'Potato Clock'.

5: 1: T6: to read a number of poems by significant poets and identify what is distinctive about the style or content of their poems

5: 1: T7: to analyse and compare poetic style, use of forms and the themes of significant poets; to respond to shades of meaning

5: 1: T8: to investigate and collect different examples of wordplay, relating form to meaning

The New Poem (for 18 words)

difficult to make sense of sentence and explain it

idea of words 'getting used to things'

New words
Should be used to being
Where they have not yet got.
So this is the poem.

addition of a comma makes it easier to make sense of the sentence

This poem is the words,
So new, have yet
Not got used to being.
Where should they be?

is there a common idea in each stanza? are there similarities in how the words are used?

this stanza explains the poem and helps the reader to appreciate the previous stanzas – it shows us the significance of where words are placed during the process of writing a poem

This poem is so new
The words have not yet
Got used to being
Where they should be.

Roger McGough

5: 1: S1: investigate word order by examining how far the order of words in sentences can be changed:
● which words are essential to meaning
● which can be deleted without damaging the basic meaning
● which words or groups of words can be moved into a different order

5: 1: S6: to understand the need for punctuation as an aid to the reader, e.g. commas to mark grammatical boundaries; a colon to signal, e.g. a list

Sky Day Dream and Homeweb *Poems 1 and 2*
by Robert Froman

Background
Robert Froman is one of the greatest concrete poets and says his poems 'began as a sort of free-wheeling haiku'. His concrete poems are well-written lines that are then shaped on the page, weaving the subject matter with wordplay. This provides the reader with an innovative way of seeing something. In these two examples, he presents crows and spiders. Other poems include the cutting of grass and slamming of doors. His poems are short, making them a good model from which children can begin to explore the concrete shaping of their own lines of poetry.

Shared reading and discussing the text
● Don't read these two poems – show them to the children and give them time to figure out what is going on. Tell them beforehand that you want them to look in silence at the page. After they have done this for a few minutes, ask them to share with a partner what they can see taking place in these poems.

● Read the poems with the children and ask them how these texts differ from most other texts they have read. Explain that the words in concrete poems are arranged on the page in a way that denotes the content. Ask them to point out how this can be seen in the poems here. In what ways do the poems look like their subjects? This can extend into considering how the poems might change in appearance if their subject matter were altered in some way, for example if the crows swooped down from the sky and then flew away again, or if the spider's web were suddenly broken by an object like a duster.

● Help the children to see how each poem can be split into two parts – visually and by content. Each poem has two thoughts. Annotate each poem, showing the children's responses to its different parts.

● Re-read the poems, listening for the musical quality of the lines. Try reading them as a group in a way that captures this.

● On each poem, draw arrows to show the direction in which the reader has to navigate the text. Can the children see how this is very different from the strategies used in regular print? Explain how the reader is aided in deciphering the text through the layout having a direction of its own – the reader can then find the route by which the words and lines make sense.

Activities
● Both texts have nature as their theme, represented as concrete poetry. Drawing on work they have done in science, can the children create their own concrete poem? Note that Froman's poems are not just words squashed into the shape of the subject – a form of concrete poetry children sometimes end up doing if they haven't seen enough good examples. These are sentences broken up to create the lines of the image they draw – the wings of the birds in flight, the spider's web and the spider's legs.

● Ask the children to create sentences using the word *but* in the middle, as in the second poem. Encourage them to work out ways in which the first clause can be reversed in an amusing way. Examples could include: *My bedroom may be a mess but... You may be the teacher but... It's raining outside but... There's a monster in the garden but... The shop window had toys that talked but...*

● Froman has come up with beautiful titles here. Write *Sky Day Dream* and *Homeweb* on a large sheet of white paper and ask the children to contribute their own thoughts about the titles, writing around the edges of the paper. They needn't be directly connected to the poem (for example, one child commented, *homeweb sounds like 'homework'*).

Extension/further reading
Children could read more poems by Robert Froman in *Seeing Things* (Grasshopper Books).

5: 1: T6: to read a number of poems by significant poets and identify what is distinctive about the style or content of their poems

5: 1: T7: to analyse and compare poetic style, use of forms and the themes of significant poets; to respond to shades of meaning; to explain and justify personal tastes; to consider the impact of full rhymes, half rhymes, internal rhymes and other sound patterns

shape of poems make them distinctive

the poems look like the subject they are about

SKY DAY DREAM

WITH THEM

COULD FLY OFF

I WISHED THAT I

INTO THE SKY

FLY OFF

SOME CROWS

ONCE I SAW

Robert Froman

how would the poem look if the birds swooped down and then took off again?

feelings conveyed by poems:

poet has a sense of yearning – he wishes that he could fly off with the birds

similarity between poems:

each poem consists of 2 parts

each part contains a different thought

reader has to work out the direction in which to read

HOMEWEB

A COBWEB MAY LOOK MESSY

BUT TO SOME SPI- DER IT IS HOME

Robert Froman

poet feels sensitive towards the spider – the web may be a nuisance to people but it is the spider's home

how would the poem look if a duster scattered the cobweb?

5: 1: T8: to investigate and collect different examples of wordplay, relating form to meaning

5: 1: T16: to convey feelings, reflections or moods in a poem through the careful choice of words and phrases

If the Earth

by Joe Miller

Background

'If the Earth' is the opening poem in *Can you Hear?* – a collection of poems raising issues about famine, war and environmental concerns. The shape of the poem is ideal for guiding us to apply the shape to the subject matter, form to meaning – and it was in this way that it was first brought to prominence in the mid-70s. Joe Miller was a mystic and teacher who lived in San Francisco.

Shared reading and discussing the text

● Hold the text at a distance and ask the children what they think the poem may be about. They won't be able to read the words but will hazard a guess based on the shape. Gather their ideas, then read the first line to them. It is as we read the title/first line that we come to link the shape to the subject – a vital trick played on the readers of concrete poetry.

● Read through the text and ask the children to focus on the first two sentences. Ask them to identify the scenario the poem is presenting. Explore the theme of the poem by asking *How is the Earth being pictured?* Once they have visualised the image of the Earth in a field (you will need to translate *a few feet*), ask them to read on, listing the wonders people would behold. Underline phrases describing each wonder: *big pools of water, little pools, water flowing between the pools*, and so on.

● Look through the poem and find the features of the Earth that are presented in new and interesting ways. The poem is picking apart the subject of the Earth and making the reader work harder to identify the features of the Earth that are mentioned. Circle words and phrases that are integral to this (for example *creatures walking*). What is Miller referring to when he uses such language?

● Locate the use of commas in the poem. Some are used to separate clauses (as in the first sentence), others to separate listed items (*they would somehow know their own lives, their own roundness*).

● Looking at the second half of the poem, ask the children to seek out the difference between how the poet thinks the Earth would be viewed in this scenario and how it is treated in reality. The poet offers the idea that we would respect the Earth more if it were this fantastic exhibit, rather than it being something that is taken for granted. Can the children circle approximately ten key words and phrases in the second half of the poem that give the essence of how people would view the Earth in this context?

Activities

● Ask the children to write a recount of a school trip to see 'The First Wonders of the World'. They should imagine that they are viewing the Earth from above, looking down on oceans, mountains, deserts, volcanoes, and so on. How would they recount what they have seen? Can they write their text within the outline of a circle?

● Ask the children to write their own *If the Earth were…* ideas. They will need to devise a scenario for it, for example *If the Earth were a special effect in a film,… If the Earth were a place you paid £100 to visit,…* Reinforce the use of the comma after this first clause and ask them to construct second clauses showing how their imaginary scenario would affect the way the Earth is treated.

Extension/further reading

This poem can be linked effectively with the theme of sustainability and provides an insight into the issue from a poetic point of view.

shape of the poem makes the reader think of the Earth – this is confirmed in the title

theme of poem – a central idea

an example of how a poem picks apart an idea

If the Earth

If   the   Earth
were only a few feet in diameter,
floating a few feet above a field somewhere,
people would come from everywhere to marvel
at it. People would walk around it, marvelling at its
big pools of water, its little pools and the water flowing
between the pools. People would marvel at the bumps on
it, and the holes in it, and they would marvel at the very thin
layer of gas surrounding it and the water suspended in the gas.
The people would marvel at all the creatures walking around
the surface of the ball, and at the creatures in the water. The
people would declare it as sacred because it was the only one,
and they would protect it so that it would not be hurt. The
ball would be the greatest wonder known, and people would
come to pray to it, to be healed, to gain knowledge, to know
beauty and to wonder how it could be. People would
love it, and defend it with their lives because they
would somehow know that their lives, their own
roundness, could be nothing without it. If
the Earth were only a few feet in
diameter.

Joe Miller

familiar things are presented in a new way (makes reader work harder)

the things people would do – consider why their attitude would be so different to what it is in reality

is this like the real Earth?

comma before an additional phrase

idea put forward at the beginning of the poem is returned to at the end

Martian Mama

by Terry Halligan

Background

A sketch – a short play lasting minutes, or even seconds – is usually built around one joke and has a small number of characters. Sketch shows have become a common feature of television comedy. This example is from a collection of sketches written by Terry Halligan specifically for children. His sketches involve the minimum of props and scenery. This is one of his 'blackout sketches', which he describes as 'wonderful quickies to do in the classroom or between longer skits in a show. They're a little like the vaudeville numbers that used to be performed in front of the curtain while the stage was being set up for the next act'.

Shared reading and discussing the text

● Briefly explain the various features of a playscript: the characters listed at the beginning, the setting of the scene, the stage directions and the way names of speakers are in capitals followed by the lines they speak.

● Read through the sketch, explaining to the children that the joke here is a surprise to the audience. Can they detect the nature of the surprise and how it is concealed until the end? Chart how the reader will respond at different stages during the reading of the script. What thoughts will they have halfway through? Write these on the text. What will be their response when they encounter the last line? Note the way in which tension is built up as Junior gets progressively more demanding. How does the final line link to what parents sometimes say to children (*I've only got one pair of hands!*)?

● Explain the concept of a sketch to the children and ask them if they can think of examples from comedy shows or children's television. If they can quote examples, ask them if they can state, in one sentence, what the main joke was within the sketch.

● Returning to how the playscript is set out, point out that such a script doesn't just contain dialogue. Ask the children if they can pick out the other parts and, as they point them out, circle them and note what they are. They should detect

the character list, the two paragraphs explaining the details of Mama's costume (*Setting the Stage*), the note in the box, the description of the scene, the stage directions in italic and the word BLACKOUT at the end. Make sure that the children understand the function of each playscript convention.

● Explore the character list and *Setting the Stage* section more closely, asking the children what they think the two aliens (mother and toddler) would look like. What sort of costumes would they wear? How would their faces be made up? How would they speak? And how would the ideal set for this sketch be arranged?

Activities

● Ask the children to look through some joke books for jokes which are told as dialogue, for example:

PERSON 1: Why do bees hum?
PERSON 2: Because they don't know the words.

JOE: My dog has no nose.
ANNA: How does he smell?
JOE: Terrible!

Can they build the jokes they find into improvised sketches, bringing the characters to life?

● Ask the children to make notes about the character of Junior by annotating copies of the text. What can they tell about his character from the things he says and does?

● Ask the children to annotate their scripts, highlighting stage directions and noting down ways in which lines can be spoken, in preparation for a performance of the extract.

● Can the children imagine other Martian scenarios involving a mother and child, or other family members, developing them into a script?

Extension/further reading

Look at sketches from current comedy programmes. Encourage the children to make quick notes about who the characters were and what the jokes entailed.

5: 1: T5: to understand dramatic conventions including:
● the conventions of scripting (e.g. stage directions, asides)
● how character can be communicated in words and gesture
● how tension can be built up through pace, silences and delivery

5: 1: T18: write own playscript, applying conventions learned from reading; include production notes

conventions of scripts:

characters

scene setting

stage directions

name of character

dialogue

MARTIAN MAMA

Blackout Sketch

Characters
MARTIAN MAMA
MARTIAN JUNIOR

Setting the Stage
The only essential part of the costume is an extra set of arms pinned under Mama's regular arms. You can make these arms from sleeves of old clothes stuffed with newspaper.

Note: *This sketch can be changed easily to suit any kind of alien or monster. Just change the names of the foods.*

SCENE. MAMA *is washing dishes, with her back turned to the audience.* JUNIOR *is sitting in a high chair eating dinner. The audience can't see Mama's extra arms because her back is turned.*

JUNIOR. Mama, I want something to drink! Gimme something to drink! (*He pounds his fists on his tray.*)

MAMA. I just did, Junior. It's right in front of you, dear.

JUNIOR (*picks up a glass of green-coloured water*). Gimme some moon-cheese pie, and more asteroid pudding, too. Come on, gimme it!

MAMA. Just a minute. Can't you see I'm busy with these dishes?

JUNIOR (*throws his water on the floor*). Uh-oh, Mama, my comet juice spilled. Hurry, clean it up! Mama, I want my dessert! Gimme my dessert!

MAMA (*turns around, revealing her four arms*). I can't do everything! I only have four arms!

BLACKOUT

the joke is built up through the script

the character is conveyed through his words and gestures

tension built up – Junior gets worse and worse until Mama reveals her arms in the final joke

5: 1: T19: to annotate a section of playscript as a preparation for performance, taking into account pace, movement, gesture and delivery of lines and the needs of the audience

5: 1: T20: to evaluate the script and the performance for their dramatic interest and impact

Krindlekrax playscript

by Philip Ridley

Background

This extract is taken from Philip Ridley's adaptation of his own story, *Krindlekrax*. It preserves all the humour displayed in the characterisation in the original text but being a playscript the action now has to be moved along by the dialogue only. In this extract, Elvis Cave has just kicked a ball – one that originally belonged to Ruskin and which he took from him – through a window of Ruskin's parents' house. Elvis is a bully who goes to the same school as Ruskin and is later chosen to play the part of the hero because of his muscular physical appearance (though fortunes change as the story draws to its conclusion).

Shared reading and discussing the text

● Draw the children's attention to the playscript conventions – the scene setting notes, the details about the characters, the use of a bold typeface to denote the speakers, and the inclusion of stage directions.

● Read through the character notes at the start of the playscript extract. Ask the children to compare these with the text (see page 10) which describes Ruskin's character in the opening of the novel. What similarities can they see between these characters? What differences? Point out the stage directions. Go through the actions performed by each character.

● Read the text at the very beginning that outlines the scene and ask the children to guess what has taken place here. How would a football end up in the middle of a table? Where might it have come from? Having done this, read through the scene. Can they form an opinion about what

sort of person Elvis may be and why there has been a succession of broken windows?

● Explore the dynamic between the characters in this extract. What is important to Ruskin? What is important to his mum? What about his dad? How does the way they ignore his excitement tie in with Mr Lace's discouraging tone in the opening extract of *Krindlekrax* (see page 10)?

Activities

● Compare this script with other ways in which speech can be represented. Take a line like Ruskin's *Morning, Mum* and model the presentation of this as direct speech (*Ruskin said, 'Morning, Mum'*) and reported speech (*Ruskin said good morning to his mum*). Can the children try representing other scripted pieces of speech in these ways?

● Drawing on the way the playscript uses dialogue to tell a story, letting the characters tell us the things that have taken place or are taking place, the children could write their own scripts. Explain that in their scripts it should be evident that a number of events have taken place through the conversation that the characters have. It is the task of their characters to allow the reader to gather what is happening and piece together a picture in their minds.

● Ask the children to create notes about the characters that they have devised, similar to the information given in this playscript extract. Before the character first appears in the scene, they should indicate what he or she is like; they may also wish to include notes on what the character is doing.

5: 1: T3: to investigate how characters are presented, referring to the text:
- through dialogue, action and description
- how the reader responds to them (as victims, heroes, etc.)
- through examining their relationships with other characters

plays can be broken into separate scenes for various settings

scene title

setting the scene

character details:
actions
age
appearance

bold typeface to differentiate speaker from speech

characterisation: the things characters say show something about them

scene opens and raises questions about what has happened

stage directions explain a character's actions

notes on the characters can also show how they react and feel

do they notice what he says? characters are preoccupied with different things

Krindlekrax playscript

Scene Three

RUSKIN'S KITCHEN

Sunlight illuminates cooker, fridge, chairs and table. A football lies in the middle of table and has obviously smashed much cutlery (including many plates of toast) and knocked toaster to the floor.

Wendy Splinter is picking up toaster. She is thirty-three years old and wearing a (faded 'n' frayed) green dressing gown, fluffy green slippers and round rimmed spectacles. She is pale, thin and has frizzy, red hair.

Winston Splinter, her husband, is huddled beside the cooker, trembling with fear. He is thirty-five years old and is wearing (green and white) pyjama bottoms, string vest, green socks and round rimmed spectacles. He is pale, thin and balding (what hair remains is frizzy and red).

Wendy Look at the mess! If the toaster's damaged… well, we can't afford a new one, you know.

Winston Not my fault.

Wendy Someone's got to do something about Elvis.

Puts bread in toaster.

We'll have no windows left at this rate.

Ruskin enters, now wearing green shorts, a striped (green and white) T-shirt and green, lace-up shoes. He is clutching satchel, sword and shield.

Ruskin Morning, Mum.

Kisses Wendy.

Wendy Mind where you tread! Elvis is up to his tricks again.

Ruskin So I see. Morning, Dad.

Winston Not my fault.

Ruskin Well… today's the day, everyone.

Removes broken crockery from seat and sits.

Wendy Tea?

Pours cup of tea for Ruskin.

Ruskin I've learnt all my lines.

Wendy That's the third window we've lost this month, Winston! I'm still finding glass in the living room. And as for the bathroom… well, no privacy there!

Winston Not my fault.

Takes can of lager from fridge.

5: 1: T5: to understand dramatic conventions including:
- the conventions of scripting (e.g. stage directions, asides)
- how character can be communicated in words and gesture
- how tension can be built up through pace, silences and delivery

5: 1: T18: write own playscript, applying conventions learned from reading; include production notes

Dear Brutus

by JM Barrie

Background

Children will be familiar with the name Peter Pan and may know the name of the author of the classic story. JM Barrie was interested in dream worlds and the passage of time. In this play, characters at an Edwardian country house party are confronted with the magical wood that moves around the country. On entering it, they step out of time and live new lives in which their real selves come to the fore, only to then return and leave the magic behind. Here we see the mysterious way in which Lob lures the characters into the Midsummer Night's wood – though he may appear to be doing the very opposite.

Children will enjoy trying out this Edwardian conversation and it is worth noting Barrie's use of stage directions. Playscripts can sometimes be hard to read – they are, after all, written for performing. In his plays, Barrie's advice about how lines should be spoken makes his playscripts excellent for reading as well as performing.

Note: Philomela (see line 22) was a tragic character from Greek mythology who had her tongue cut out, caused a king to eat his son and ended up being turned into a nightingale. Purdie is referring to nightingales but with the old mythic name, Philomel, restored in an equally mythical wood.

Shared reading and discussing the text

● Set the scene, explaining the background, and then read the first two pieces of dialogue (in which Purdie and Lob introduce the idea of the wood). Underline the words *pout* and *credulous*. Ask the children what they think these words might mean. Look the words up in a dictionary and, revisiting Lob's words, ask the children if they can see why he may give a *pout for the credulous*.

● Read through to the end of the extract. Look at the different attitudes the characters exhibit in discussing the *sporting wood*. Focus on Lob and Purdie, and on the board create two columns in which words that describe their differing responses can be recorded. Ask the children to describe the response and then, for each

character, draw three or more reasons from the text to justify their inferences. Begin with Purdie. Look at the way he encourages Lob's telling of the story, the words he uses to describe the wood and the plan he has for the evening. Switch to Lob, looking at the way in which he talks about the wood and the evening ahead.

● Underline the adverbial directions used to indicate how lines are to be spoken (*waggishly, grandly, doubtfully*). Make a list of these and define what they mean. Take the children through these lines, asking them to try delivering them in the manner indicated.

Activities

● Purdie encourages Lob to retell the story and Coade uses reported speech to recall Lob's opinion. Ask the children to devise an alternative scene in which Caroline and Joanna tell a third character of the conversation described here, again using reported speech. They could do this as a drama activity, recounting the scene, and then write a playscript in which the characters relate the conversation, for example *Mr Purdie said that Lob had told him… Lob told us he thought it was all nonsense…* and so on.

● Revisit the use of adverbs in stage directions. Ask the children to make a list of adverbs that could describe the nature of a conversation. Steer them away from regular speech adverbs, such as *happily* and *loudly*, towards more interesting ones, such as *uncertainly* and *deviously*. They can draw upon dictionaries to resource this task. Ask them to try writing their own dialogue between two characters, the guiding principle being that they must use this new group of adverbs. They could then try acting it out.

Extension/further reading

This is a story of Edwardians on night-time visits to a place where time stands still and people behave in strange and savage ways. Look again at the story of Peter Pan for parallels. Encourage the children to read other JM Barrie plays – *The Admirable Crichton* involves Edwardians being thrown into unfamiliar circumstances.

5: 1: T5: to understand dramatic conventions including:
● the conventions of scripting (e.g. stage directions, asides)
● how character can be communicated in words and gesture
● how tension can be built up through pace, silences and delivery

5: 1: T9: to develop an active attitude towards reading: seeking answers, anticipating events, empathising with characters and imagining events that are described

5: 1: T18: write own playscript, applying conventions learned from reading; include production notes

how will a speaker do these? what do they mean?

DEAR BRUTUS

PURDIE.   Tell them what you told us, Lob.

LOB (*with a pout for the credulous*).   It is all nonsense, of course; just foolish talk of the villagers. They say that on Midsummer Eve there is a strange wood in this part of the country.

ALICE (*lowering*).   Where?

PURDIE.   Ah, that is one of its most charming features. It is never twice in the same place apparently. It has been seen on different parts of the Downs and on More Common; once it was close to Radley village and another time about a mile from the sea. Oh, a sporting wood!

LADY CAROLINE.   And Lob is anxious that we should all go and look for it?

COADE.   Not he; Lob is the only sceptic in the house. Says it is all rubbish, and that we shall be sillies if we go. But we believe, eh, Purdie?

PURDIE (*waggishly*).   Rather!

LOB (*the artful*).   Just wasting the evening. Let us have a round game at cards here instead.

PURDIE (*grandly*).   No, sir, I am going to find that wood.

JOANNA.   What is the good of it when it is found?

PURDIE.   We shall wander in it deliciously, listening to a new sort of bird called the Philomel.

   (LOB *is behaving in the most exemplary manner; making sweet little clucking sounds.*)

JOANNA (*doubtfully*).   Shall we keep together, Mr. Purdie?

PURDIE.   No, we must hunt in pairs.

JOANNA (*converted*).   I think it would be rather fun.

character conveyed by words and gestures

way of speaking is different from speech today

building up tension – how do Lob, Purdie, Coade and Joanna react to the wood?

directions guide the speaker

5: 1: S5: to understand the difference between direct and reported speech (e.g. *she said, 'I am going', she said she was going*), e.g. through:
● finding and comparing examples from reading
● discussing contexts and reasons for using particular forms and their effects
● transforming direct into reported speech and vice versa, noting changes in punctuation and words that have to be changed or added

5: 1: W10: to use adverbs to qualify verbs in writing dialogue, e.g. *timidly, gruffly, excitedly*, using a thesaurus to extend vocabulary

A Little Bit From the Author by Paul Jennings

Background

Paul Jennings was a teacher and his stories draw upon the sorts of experiences that can often happen with Year 5 children. However, he puts a slant on them that brings in the magical and bizarre. In the earlier editions of his short story collections, Jennings would always end with 'A Little Bit From the Author', in which he would give the experience that led him to write a particular story.

Shared reading and discussing the text

● Read through the autobiographical recount and ask the children if they have ever had an experience that left them feeling guilty. Some may even be prepared to tell you more! Remind the children of the extract from *The Gizmo* (page 16) in which they read about the trick the gadget played on the boy who stole it. Jennings wrote the book as a link to his past experiences, likening the gizmo to a guilty conscience.

● Look through the text, annotating the features that show it is a recount. There is the opening line that grabs the reader's attention and introduces the subject matter, orientating the reader. The text shows chronological sequence with connective words signalling the passage of time and one thing causing another. Additional details, such as thoughts and feelings, fill out the narrative. There are also the specific details – ages and prices – that root the autobiography and make it realistic.

● When did this happen and who was involved? Focusing on the first paragraph, can the children list the information given? Establish that in only three sentences the reader can place the event in time, figure out who was there and understand what the main body of the recount is very likely to be about.

● How would the children split the story into three or four sections? Ask them to mark these

off mentally (the stealing of the hair pins, the hosepipe incident and the contemplating of the guilty conscience which led to the writing of his book) and then gather some of their ideas, annotating the text.

● What indications are there that this is an informal anecdote? Ask the children to look through the text, finding words or phrases that make it sound like a person speaking to the reader. Explain that words and phrases like *Well* and *I guess* and *I felt so bad* help to develop an informal tone.

● Ask the children to circle the connective words that show the different times things took place. The passage of time is recorded in an interesting way in this recount, chronicling two events separated by some years.

Activities

● Ask the children to write their own recount of a time when they did something that left them feeling guilty. They might, or might not, have owned up. Encourage them to make sure that they orientate the reader and convey time, making use of connectives. Can they also use an informal tone? They should try to convey how they felt during the episode they are recounting.

● In *The Gizmo,* Jennings takes a mundane event and uses it as the springboard for a fantastic tale of cross-dressing. Ask the children to look at their own recount and devise a magical or bizarre slant upon the experience they had. They can then use this to plan a short story.

Extension/further reading

The author is *always on the lookout for* small things in his life, *little events*, that he can use in his writing. Ask the children to do the same (perhaps writing down notes in their daily lives), so that they can draw upon their own memories to use in their story writing.

5: 1: T4: to consider how texts can be rooted in the writer's experience, e.g. historical events and places, experience of wartime, friendship, holidays

5: 1: T24: to write recounts based on subject, topic or personal experiences for (a) a close friend and (b) an unknown reader, e.g. an account of a field trip, a match, a historical event

opening line grabs the reader's attention and tells us the subject of the whole recount

informal style similar to how a speaker would tell these events

insight into thoughts and feelings of people in the recount

text can be divided into separate sections based on different events

writers can use a small thing that happens in their lives as the basis for a story

details orientate the reader

connective word signalling how one thing causes another

passage of time

insight into thoughts and feelings of people in the recount

how texts can be rooted in the writer's experience

A Little Bit From the Author

I have only stolen something once in my life. I was six years old and I took a packet of hair pins from the lounge-room of the lady next door. They would have been worth about twenty cents, I guess.

That type of hair pin was only used by girls and women so I gave them to my mother. I also told a lie. I said, "Look what I found on the footpath, Mum."

Well, she was so pleased. "Oh, you are a good boy," she said. "That's just what I need." She went on and on and on about how clever and kind I was. The more she said the worse I felt. My conscience really gave me a bad time. The thought that I had done something wrong just wouldn't go away and it made me unhappy for ages. I was a thief. I felt so bad that I have never forgotten the incident.

When I was a teacher some of my students were talked into stealing a hosepipe by some big boys. They didn't know what to do with the hosepipe and in the end they threw it in a pond. Someone saw them and came and reported it to the school. They had to buy a new hosepipe and say sorry to the owner.

Both of these things happened a long time ago. But last year I got to thinking about a guilty conscience. And how some people talk other people into stealing. It seemed like good material for a book.

So I wrote a book called *The Gizmo* about a boy who steals a gadget from the market. He throws it away but it follows him around. Like a guilty conscience.

These little events are the stuff of stories. I am always on the lookout for them.

5: 1: T21: to identify the features of recounted texts such as sports reports, diaries, police reports, including:
- introduction to orientate reader
- chronological sequence
- degree of formality adopted
- use of connectives, e.g. *first... next... once*

Willy the Warthog by Paul Sussman

Background

The sale of the *Big Issue* paper is a common sight in most city centres. In its early days Paul Sussman's section, in which this text originally appeared, included bizarre news stories from around the world. They included horrific deaths, such as the chef skewered by spaghetti whirled round in a freak wind, and weird situations, such as the car that rolled into the door of a phone box, trapping its owner for three days. Of course, there was never a disclaimer and the stories were presented as items of news.

Shared reading and discussing the text

● Read part of the first sentence of the text (up to *culminated in him*) and ask the children if they can guess what is coming. Then read the rest of the sentence and explain the concept of animal rights. Ask the children if they can see how a caretaker could end up shooting a visitor in the buttock. Explain that this is a news story from the *Big Issue*. Point out that news stories can be of worldwide importance; other stories can be human interest or of a bizarre personal nature, this one being an example of the latter. They might be able to recall stories they have seen on the news within this category. The first sentence has orientated the reader – what questions will the reader now have that will make them want to read further?

● Read the text and annotate the features that let us know it is a recount. There is the opening sentence to orientate the reader, the connectives that show the passage of time, details to fill out the facts of the story and, in this instance as it is a news story, an appropriate level of formality.

● Note the sequence of events. Look at the way in which the story is built up, from a start in which we are given a précis of the tale, to the more developed details. We read the first lines and wonder how the shooting could have occurred. As we read on, we discover the mistake that was made.

● Point out the quotes from Lawrence Bilbo and the caretaker Albert Miggins that are given in the text. These help the reader to learn more about the people involved. Ask the children to imagine the words of the caretaker or a passing teacher after the event. In shared writing, write what they think the person would say. Draw the children's attention to correct punctuation when using direct speech.

● Ask the children to tell you which of the more difficult words they liked. Search for interesting adjectives and circle them (for example, *lacerated*) or powerful and evocative verbs (for example, *pursued*). Can they retell sections of the story in ways that simplify the vocabulary?

● Explain that stories are sometimes presented as news, with little truth to them. Stories on April Fool's Day or in certain tabloids can fall into this category. Do the children think this story is true? Ask them to give reasons for and against the truthfulness of this news item.

Activities

● In the *'a lion or something'* quote there is an interesting example of direct speech being placed within text that is reported (*convinced he was actually*). Taking quotes from the text and using the ones they have created themselves, the children could rewrite sentences that include direct speech and turn them into reported speech.

● Ask the children to create their own 'Can you believe this?' story. It needs to be on the fringes of the believable – so monsters and aliens are out. They might want to imagine embarrassing or bizarre things that could happen at school (teacher anecdotes might help in this respect).

Extension/further reading

Encourage the children to look for books of bizarre facts (on a 'crazy but true' theme) in the local library or school library, collating their favourites.

5: 1: T21: to identify the features of recounted texts such as sports reports, diaries, police reports, including:
- introduction to orientate reader
- chronological sequence
- degree of formality adopted
- use of connectives, e.g. *first... next... once*

5: 1: T24: to write recounts based on subject, topic or personal experiences for (a) a close friend and (b) an unknown reader, e.g. an account of a field trip, a match, a historical event

5: 1: S7: from reading, to understand how dialogue is set out, e.g. on separate lines for alternate speakers in narrative, and the positioning of commas before speech marks

opening words orientate the reader: what happened? who to?

language used to develop interest: adjectives

level of formality involved in recounting news

quotes give the reader impressions of incident from people involved

language used to develop interest: verbs

Willy the Warthog

One of the most disastrous school talks of all time was given by American Lawrence Bilbo, whose lecture on 'Why We Shouldn't be Cruel to Animals' culminated in him being shot in the buttock by a belligerent caretaker. An ardent animal rights campaigner, Mr Bilbo, 36, travelled the length and breadth of America giving talks to schoolchildren on animal welfare. "I used to dress up as Willy the Warthog," explained the caring conservationist. "I had a furry brown costume, and tusks, and little trotters that I wore over my shoes like galoshes. It gave the whole lecture a bit of topicality and the children loved it." On the day in question, Mr Bilbo had arrived to give a talk at a school in Cruger, Mississippi, secreting himself in the toilet and donning his Willy the Warthog costume before scampering into the corridor with a loud snort, ready to address the school's 200 children. Unfortunately, he was spotted by short-sighted caretaker Albert Miggins, who, convinced he was actually 'a lion or something', fetched his shotgun and pursued a terrified Mr Bilbo into the school playground, where he shot him in the backside. The lacerated lecturer has since discarded his warthog costume in favour of a bright-orange three-piece suit. "It's safer that way," he explained.

level of formality involved in recounting news

details support the reader's understanding

why might this lead to Bilbo being shot in the buttock?

chronological sequence: recount gives background to the event, then details after the event happened

temporal connective words show passage of time and give chronological sequence

5: 1: S4: to adapt writing for different readers and purposes by changing vocabulary, tone and sentence structures to suit, e.g. simplifying for younger readers

5: 1: S5: to understand the difference between direct and reported speech (e.g. *she said, 'I am going', she said she was going*), e.g. through:
- finding and comparing examples from reading
- discussing contexts and reasons for using particular forms and their effects
- transforming direct into reported speech and vice versa, noting changes in punctuation and words that have to be changed or added

5: 1: S8: to revise and extend work on verbs

Unhappy ending for the newborn hippo

Background

In this text the basic features of news reporting are presented in a clear way (headline, picture, caption, recount of events, and so on). In some news reports, maps and diagrams are used to clarify information, but here the detail – about a complex rescue attempt – is communicated through the text. As with many prominent news stories, a photograph reinforces the realism of the event. Another common feature of news reports is that the nature of the subject matter – in this case, the keeping of animals in captivity – can prompt people to respond in a variety of ways.

Shared reading and discussing the text

● Read the first sentence and ask the children to tell you the facts we are given. Establish that a great deal has been said within just one sentence. The beginning not only grabs the reader's attention but gives the main thrust of what the story is going to be about. Editors know that readers have a tendency to skim the text, once the first one or two sentences have been read, so the opening lines have to have the essential information packed into them in a condensed form.

● The first paragraph of a news story communicates further general information that is relevant to the story, aiming to answer main questions, such as who…?, what…?, when…?, where…? and why…? Ask the children to think of questions that could have been answered by the first paragraph here, for example *What happened to the hippo?* Make a list of these. Annotate the points at which they are answered within the first paragraph of the news story.

● Locate the specific features of this news report – headline, picture and caption, first line giving main details, quotations from people involved – in addition to the basic elements of a recount (chronological sequence with appropriate connectives, degree of formality appropriate to news reporting, and so on).

● Ask the children to read through the text and list the various measures taken to try to save the baby hippo. Drawing a line on the board, map out the various interventions and the order in which they were tried. Point out the structure of this part of the story: the complication (several episodes) followed by the resolution (albeit a sad one).

● Look at the quotes in the text, asking the children to read them silently and consider what these snippets of direct speech add to the story. Discuss the emotion communicated. There isn't a quote from any members of the fire brigade – can the children write down what one of them could have said?

Activities

● Ask the children to imagine they are preparing a news report on this story for television news. Can they write their own script for it?

● The headline is too long. Can the children come up with a number of alternative headlines and then choose the best from their list? Stress that they need to keep it shorter than the example given.

● Give the children the task of preparing their own idea for a news story set in a safari park. They can begin by making the notes they would gather as a reporter, including details and quotes, and then plan and write their own news report. Point out that their ending can be a happy one (unlike the story about the hippo).

● Ask the children to cut 60 words from the story, as if they were editing the paper. Explain that they will have to seek out words or sentences that can be considered of least use, and that rephrasing of sentences may be necessary. As they do this, remind them of the importance of communicating a full and clear news recount.

Extension/further reading

The baby hippo died in a safari park, not in the wild. However, had the baby been in a similar situation in the wild there would have been no fire brigade to attempt a rescue. Re-read the last quote to the children to stimulate discussion on how humane it is to keep animals in captivity.

5: 1: **T21:** to identify the features of recounted texts such as sports reports, diaries, police reports, including:
● introduction to orientate reader
● chronological sequence
● degree of formality adopted
● use of connectives, e.g. *first… next… once*

5: 1: **S1:** investigate word order by examining how far the order of words in sentences can be changed:
● which words are essential to meaning
● which can be deleted without damaging the basic meaning
● which words or groups of words can be moved into a different order

news story features:
headline

Unhappy ending for the newborn hippo rescued from a lake

long headline but tells us about the story in less than 1 sentence

Exhausted: The baby hippo perched at the side of the water

picture

caption

1st sentence

opening sentence gives the main points of the story: who is involved where it took place what has happened

THE newborn hippo rescued from a rain-swollen lake has died, despite the best efforts of its mother and the fire brigade.
The 18in high calf was delivered on a ledge at the side of the lake by its mother, Bar-Bel, but kept slipping into the water.
Bar-Bel desperately tried to nudge her baby to safety. When she failed, the keepers at West Midlands Safari Park called in the fire brigade.
They pumped 200,000 gallons from the lake and scooped the little

hippo up in a net. The animal was then given oxygen and put under a heat lamp as it fought for life.
Yesterday, however, head warden Bob Lawrence announced that the 50lb baby had died 'in its sleep' having swallowed a large amount of water during the rescue.
"We are all very, very disappointed but the calf was just too exhausted after her ordeal," he said.
"Everything humanly possible was done to save the calf and the fire brigade did a magnificent job."

recount text gives events in chronological sequence, with phrases being linked by time and connective words such as 'then' and 'yesterday'

quotes add to a news story the feelings of those involved and opinions about what happened

5: 1: **T24:** to write recounts based on subject, topic or personal experiences for (a) a close friend and (b) an unknown reader, e.g. an account of a field trip, a match, a historical event

5: 1: **S3:** to discuss, proof-read and edit their own writing for clarity and correctness, e.g. by creating more complex sentences, using a range of connectives, simplifying clumsy constructions

Don't be a reject!

Background

Taking the instructions genre to its most officious, this government leaflet, published in 1999, tells readers about how they should apply for a photocard driving licence. With photocards it is important that usable photos are submitted (it is no good simply cutting out a head and shoulders shape from a holiday snap!). As with most government information leaflets, the aim is to provide concise instructions that can be understood by all members of the reading public.

Shared reading and discussing the text

● Read through the text and ask the children if they can see why such a leaflet may be necessary. What sorts of problems is it seeking to avert? From the text, can they list the reasons why photocard applications have been rejected in the past?

● Explore the layout of the text. Look at the different font sizes and styles. Pick out features such as words in bold, and so on. Discuss which words are emphasised and why this is so. Note particularly the bold type in the bulleted text. Why should those words be highlighted? Point out the inclusion of an example – a useful addition to an instructional text.

● Look at how the text is structured. Annotate the features of an instructional text, including the clear purpose fulfilled by the instructions and the step-by-step commands. Point out the way in which the bullet points split the text into succinct sections of information. What subtitle would the children give to each of these?

● Reading the bullet points, point out the use of an imperative verb at the start of each one. Remind the children of the nature of an imperative verb and the function it performs in telling a reader what to do.

Activities

● Ask the children to make notes about the text by recording ten key words (they will find the emphasis that the leaflet gives to certain words helpful). They can then work in pairs, with one partner using their key words to recall as much of the text as they can, and the other marking a copy of the text to see how much their partner can recollect. Once they have both tried this, suggest that the pairs work together on a definitive list of five words. They could try recalling the text from these notes on the following day.

● Can the children write their own bulleted advice leaflet? It could draw on school rules or classroom routines. They can start with a general paragraph, then move on to three specific bullet points. To do this they will need to select their information and organise it into sections, using an imperative verb to start each bullet. They may wish to use brackets, as in the example here, for additional information which will be helpful. Do their instructions work?

Extension/further reading

Encourage the children to collect other examples of public information leaflets from libraries, dentists, doctors' surgeries, and so on. Ask them to check how clearly these convey their information.

5: 1: T22: to read and evaluate a range of instructional texts in terms of their:
● purposes
● organisation and layout
● clarity and usefulness

5: 1: T25: to write instructional texts, and test them out, e.g. instructions for loading computers, design briefs for technology, rules for games

5: 1: T26: to make notes for different purposes, e.g. noting key points as a record of what has been read, listing cues for a talk, and to build on these notes in their own writing or speaking

layout makes text in title and instructions clear

different typefaces used for interest and clarity

purpose of task outlined in opening, and explanation given as to why the leaflet is important; lets reader know what problem can be averted

imperative verbs – what to do

clarity: text split up into 3 bullet points

bold text used for words and sentences that are important

reference to different sections of application form put in brackets

diagram and example given to help reader's understanding

this emphasises the formality of the text

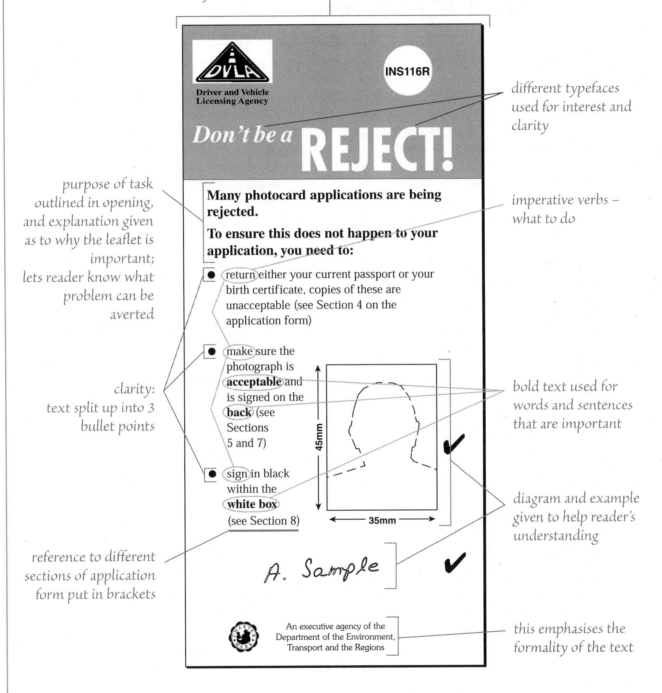

5: 1: S8: to revise and extend work on verbs (see Y4 objectives), focusing on:
● forms: active, interrogative, imperative

5: 1: S9: to identify the imperative form in instructional writing and the past tense in recounts and use this awareness when writing for these purposes

Your short story

Background

This text, which has been used as a poster in Key Stage 2 classrooms, is used to remind children of principles that they should bear in mind when planning to write a short story. Instructions like these are very much aimed at focusing the work children undertake in writing, allowing them to work towards a specific storyline and fine-tune their ideas. After using these instructions regularly, children will begin to recall the five tips without looking at them.

Shared reading and discussing the text

● Read the text, then ask the children to consider what the purpose of a poster with this text on it would be. Establish that the text can be used to inform the work of a young writer.

● Explore the structure of the text. Note the title and first sentence followed by the five points, each one having two subsidiary points (bulleted). Discuss how the bullets make the layout clearer and the text easier to understand. Ask the children to each pick out one instruction that they think they could apply to their own writing. Gather some of their responses.

● Annotate the text, underlining each of the verbs. Draw the children's attention to the imperative verbs, instructing the reader to do something (for example, *Plan... Stick... Use...*), and the use of the second person (*you, your*). Why is the imperative used in instructions? Ask the children to remodel these sentences, saying them aloud as if they were something they had already done, and using the first person and past tense (for example, *Plan your story...* should become *I planned my story...*). Can they pick out the words that change – and ones that don't – when they do this to a sentence?

Activities

● Reading their own writing and referring to the text here, can the children make some brief notes on changes they could make to improve their writing?

● Ask the children to create their own teaching poster presenting five points which should be remembered when carrying out a particular task. It could be five points to bear in mind when writing a playscript, or laying out their work on a page. For example (for the latter):

  – Make sure you have written your name and date at the top.

  – Keep your writing clear and neat.

  – Separate your writing into paragraphs of text (indent the first line). A new paragraph usually shows a change of focus, time or place.

  – Is your heading appropriate, and is it short enough?

  – Check spellings and grammar.

Extension/further reading

Sue Palmer's excellent Big Books from TTS publications show various ways in which pieces of writing can be structured, and give clear diagrams. They offer excellent examples of how to give tips to writers.

5: 1: T22: to read and evaluate a range of instructional texts in terms of their:
● purposes
● organisation and layout
● clarity and usefulness

5: 1: T25: to write instructional texts, and test them out, e.g. instructions for loading computers, design briefs for technology, rules for games

5: 1: T26: to make notes for different purposes, e.g. noting key points as a record of what has been read, listing cues for a talk, and to build on these notes in their own writing or speaking

---

general title ——— # Your short story

introduces task ——— Here are some tips for planning your short story.

Plan your beginning and your ending and the bridge between the two.

main points
● Plan your story so you know where you will be in 45 minutes.

sub points – less important than the main points
● Plan a strong middle, bridging the beginning and the end.

Make your characters workable, interesting and enjoyable.

2nd person, addressing the instruction to 'you'
● Stick to two or three characters we will know and enjoy.
● Name and describe your characters.

Let the reader know where they are.

imperative verbs
● Sense a setting (what does it look, sound and smell like?) and take your reader there.
● Use adjectives to describe the place.

Plan some dialogue.
● Use it to tell what happens in the story (for example, "The door is opening!").
● Use interesting words for "said".

Think through the thoughts and feelings.
● Let readers feel what a character feels.
● Give your characters an 'inner voice' (words that tell what we wouldn't see, for example "I realised…", "Lou was afraid that…").

examples given or phrases defined and clarified in brackets

picks up on common issues in story writing

5: 1: S8: to revise and extend work on verbs (see Y4 objectives), focusing on:
● forms: active, interrogative, imperative
● person: 1st, 2nd, 3rd. Identify and classify examples from reading; experiment with transforming tense/form/person in these examples – discuss changes that need to be made and effects on meaning

5: 1: S9: to identify the imperative form in instructional writing and the past tense in recounts and use this awareness when writing for these purposes

Pick a Book

Background

As with many books of magic tricks, this one gives the equipment and instructions and adds that crucial bit of 'patter', where the magician talks very quickly, telling the audience what magic will take place. This text explains how the magician and his assistant manage to accomplish the illusion of mind reading.

The text is structured with a clear instructions format, presenting the task in steps. Children might want to try this mind-reading trick for themselves and may be able to think of others to try out.

Shared reading and discussing the text

● Perform the trick – with a child or another adult as your assistant – before reading through the text with the class. Try the trick a few times but do not explain how it is done. Once you have done this, ask the children to get into pairs, and provide each pair with a pile of nine books and a photocopy of the text. Ask each pair to read the text at their own pace and, when they are ready, practise the trick with their accomplice.

● Read through the text and demarcate the features of an instructional text that guide a reader through an activity – the list of resources needed, the step-by-step instructions, the connectives (*Then, while*), the layout, and so on. Ask the children to identify what is special about the verbs in the text. Revise imperative verbs and their purpose.

● Magic tricks present an illusion. In this case the reader is told how the illusion is achieved (in point 4). Note the turning point in the text, when the reader becomes aware of how the trick works

(*But look very carefully at where his finger is pointing…*). Discuss with the children how the illusion is maintained (*Your assistant will carry on…*) in point 5.

● It is important that a magician talks quickly and confidently when doing a magic trick because it helps to present the illusion. Ask the children to look at point 5 in the instructions, then see if they can make up some patter that could be used at the point when the magician reveals the chosen book. They will need it to sound mysterious and magical.

Activities

● Ask the children to find out about two magic tricks from other members of staff or at home. Explain that they should make brief notes, so that they can share the tricks with the class and write their own set of instructions. These could be compiled into a class book of magic.

● Ask the children to rewrite the trick, once they have learned how it is done. They can have as many steps as they wish and vary the patter. When they have done this, compare their points with the original. In some cases children will have made two steps out of a part of a trick covered in one step in the text; in others they might have brought steps together. Encourage the children to compare different rewritings of the trick and check how clearly it has been presented.

Extension/further reading

Children could bring in their own magic books from home or from the library and try learning some new tricks. This could even develop into a class magic show.

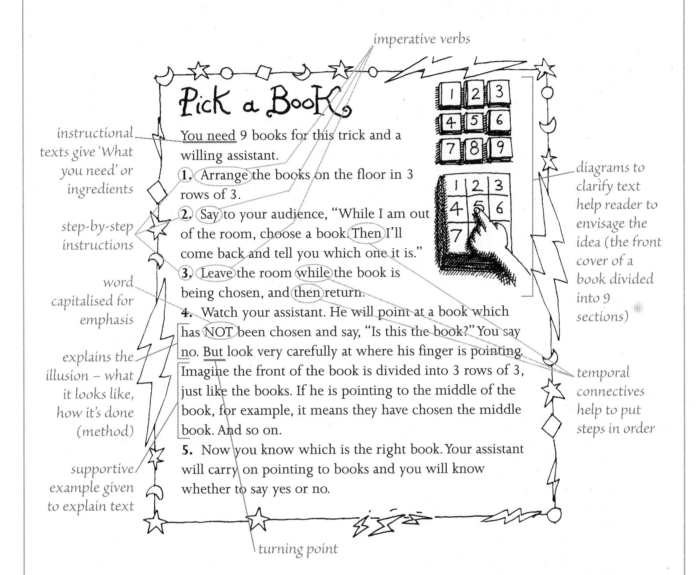

imperative verbs

Pick a Book

You need 9 books for this trick and a willing assistant.

1. Arrange the books on the floor in 3 rows of 3.

2. Say to your audience, "While I am out of the room, choose a book. Then I'll come back and tell you which one it is."

3. Leave the room while the book is being chosen, and then return.

4. Watch your assistant. He will point at a book which has NOT been chosen and say, "Is this the book?" You say no. But look very carefully at where his finger is pointing. Imagine the front of the book is divided into 3 rows of 3, just like the books. If he is pointing to the middle of the book, for example, it means they have chosen the middle book. And so on.

5. Now you know which is the right book. Your assistant will carry on pointing to books and you will know whether to say yes or no.

instructional texts give 'What you need' or ingredients

step-by-step instructions

word capitalised for emphasis

explains the illusion – what it looks like, how it's done (method)

supportive example given to explain text

diagrams to clarify text help reader to envisage the idea (the front cover of a book divided into 9 sections)

temporal connectives help to put steps in order

turning point

The Creation

retold by Sarah Quie

Background

Across a range of cultures, myths provide a way of encapsulating and explaining experience. This is an Egyptian myth of creation. A culture like Ancient Egypt, so dependent on the Nile for its life, saw the emergence of life from 'the waters' and developed a myth of creation that culminates in the provision of the river. Myths 'explain' why the world is the way it is, how things came to be as they are – how leopards gained their spots, why rain falls from the sky, why dogs chase cars, and so on.

Shared reading and discussing the text

● Point out the way in which a myth like this explains the origins of many features of creation. Read through the text and ask the children to list the nouns – proper and common – that are the most significant in the story. Write each one on a separate piece of card (*Nun, mound, Amun-Ra, phoenix bird*…). Collect enough for every child in the class to have one noun then, standing with the whole class in a circle, hold a card with the word *beginning* on it. Talk the class through the process of putting the nouns in the order in which they appear in the creation story, discussing, for example, whether the word *flower* should appear before *mound*. Having sorted the cards, let the children use them to recall the story, step by step.

● Annotate the text, showing how it starts with the darkness at the beginning of time, then how one item leads to another item being created. Encourage the children to find examples of this, and annotate the text to point out the links. Focus on the part which explains the origins of the first people – in a creation story this is often given prominence.

● Make a list of the characters that appear in this tale. In contrast to monotheistic tales in which one God does all the creating, this is a polytheistic tale, in which many gods are involved. Pick out the various gods – Shu, Tefnut, Geb, Nut and Khnum – noting their particular characteristics (god of air, goddess of dew and moisture, earth god, goddess of the sky, and the ram-headed god who could use his potter's wheel to make people out of clay).

● Ask the children to look at all the created things that are explained in this story, and make a list of them on the board. Point out the opposites – how land and water, light and dark, earth and sky, son and daughter, gods and people are created.

Activities

● Can the children draw a diagram of the story, including all the features as represented in the text? The first part of the diagram could show a mass of black water, the second part Amun-Ra in the lotus flower, emerging from the depths, the third part Amun-Ra becoming a bird. Arrows can be used to explain the order in which events take place.

● Beginning with the words *Egyptian* and *Creation*, revise the various spellings of the *suffix* sounding like 'shun'. Ask the children to look up in the dictionary other words that end in this sound, exploring the different spellings (for example *magician, cushion*). Make a collection of these words and group them under the different spellings.

● Ask the children to create their own myths to explain how the world of their experience came to exist. Looking at the things around them will help them to devise some opposites (country and city, noise and quiet, adults and children) which they can use as a focus. Remind them of the importance of building up the events, layer upon layer, so that a small familiar object, such as a seed, eventually becomes a greater familiar object, such as the world.

Extension/further reading

In RE children could explore other creation stories, such as the myths told by the Native Americans.

This story can be used as a stimulus for work in art and design. Children could include drawings of flowers appearing from watery depths and phoenix birds flying to pyramid mounds.

5: 2: T1: to identify and classify the features of myths, legends and fables, e.g. the moral in a fable, fantastical beasts in legends

5: 2: T11: to write own versions of legends, myths and fables, using structures and themes identified in reading

5: 2: W8: to recognise and spell the suffix: -*cian* etc.

myth explaining the Creation – origins of people, Egypt, Nile

according to Ancient Egyptian belief, the watery mass of chaos that existed before the world came into being

things beginning

a creator

first people

real things are explained

THE CREATION

In the beginning the black waters of Nun enveloped everything and there was darkness and silence everywhere. Then suddenly, out of the watery depths, the pointed tips of a closed lotus flower and a primeval mound appeared. Slowly, they both rose above the water until they were fully formed. The lotus flower then began to uncurl its tightly closed petals and a brilliant yellow light shone from it. When fully open it revealed the small, but perfectly formed figure of the creator, Amun-Ra, sitting in the blaze of light, surrounded by a wonderful perfume. He then turned into a beautiful phoenix bird and flew to the newly formed mound which was shaped like a pyramid. He settled down there stretching out his brightly coloured red and gold wings and gave a great cry which echoed in the silence around him.

Amun-Ra became lonely in his watery solitude and so, out of himself, he created a son, Shu, the god of air, and a daughter, the lioness-headed Tefnut, goddess of the dew and of moisture. Amun-Ra was so proud of his children that he wept with happiness.

Shu and Tefnut then conceived a son, Geb, the earth god, and a daughter, Nut, the goddess of the sky. Geb and Nut cared deeply for each other and out of their love came four children. The first was a kind and honourable son, Osiris, who was followed by his brother, Seth. Lastly, Nut gave birth to two daughters, the brave and magical Isis, and her gentle and caring sister, Nephthys. These children, unlike their ancestors, lived on earth. After them many more gods and goddesses were born.

Lastly, Amun-Ra ordered the ram-headed god, Khnum, to turn his potter's wheel and fashion man out of clay. Gently breathing life into man, Amun-Ra now realized that he required a place to live, and so he created Egypt. Just as Amun-Ra had emerged from the waters of Nun, so he created the River Nile so that Egypt and its peoples could grow and prosper.

gods take charge of different elements of creation:

earth god

sky goddess

ram-headed potter

god of air

goddess of dew and moisture

5: 2: W10: to investigate further antonyms. Why do some words have opposites, e.g. *near, over,* while others have more than one opposite, e.g. *big, right,* and others have none, e.g. *green, wall*? Investigate common spelling patterns and other ways of creating opposites through additional words and phrases. Link to children's knowledge of adjectives and adverbs

The Hunting of Death
retold by Geraldine McCaughrean

Background

In this Rwandan myth death comes into the world as a scaly creature. God loves the people of the world, so he alerts them to the existence of this threat (Death is someone who will *steal your hearbeat*) and calls upon his angels to hunt him down. This extract records how the creature Death escapes the hunters by beguiling a human – an old woman. The angel hunstmen close in on Death, but he dupes the old woman into sheltering him. Parallels may be seen with the serpent of Genesis who deceives Eve. As with many other primeval myths, this one steps beyond explaining Earth to exploring the human condition and the origins of evil.

Shared reading and discussing the text

● Set the scene of the story, telling the children why the angels are hunting Death. Read as far as the line *'But* you *wouldn't like me to be killed, would you?'*. Split the class into four groups. Ask one group to consider what, at that point, they would say to the old woman if they had been at this scene. What advice would they give? Ask another group to consider what Death is up to. Ask the third to decide what they think the woman will do. How do they think she will respond? Ask the fourth to predict how the story will end. Go through each group's thoughts in turn. Encourage each group to make any connection they can between their thoughts and those of another group (for example, the fourth group may come up with an ending that the first warned against). Read the rest of the text and discuss how close their predictions were.

● A common feature of myths is the lack of developed characters. The characters are often flat, simply performing a function – we aren't told much about Shu and Tefnut in the previous extract, for example. Ask the children how they would describe Death. Can they imagine how Death would move and what he sounds like as he speaks? Ask them to explore the ways in which he persuades the old woman. Underline examples of this, including the flattery, proposal of marriage and pleading. Then ask them to describe the old woman – what her face looks like and how she reacts. Point out the slyness and smarminess of Death and the foolishness of the old woman.

● Myths often involve an encounter between the real world in its early stages and the world of the gods. The laws of nature are yet to be formed. Ask the children to look through the extract and decide which of the two characters featured In this discussion is the more mythical figure and which appears like a real person. Many cultures feature myths that explain how bad things come into the world. Point out and annotate features in this text that are common to such myths – a god, an encounter with a human, an action by the human that causes all the problems that follow.

● In a drama session, let groups of children take the part of the narrator, the old woman, Death and the angel huntsmen. They can add to the scene in which the hunters question the woman and create new dialogue.

Activities

● Death is described by the old woman as a *flatterer*. Ask them to write a speech in which they flatter a character of their own choosing. If they look at the sort of language Death uses in the story it will help them to make their own words similarly silver-tongued.

● The story records how the initial deception of the people on Earth caused them to let Death maintain his place in the world. Other myths record the first argument or the first time people began using different languages. Ask the children to think of another aspect of human experience, such as misery, happiness or fear, and create a new myth in which it is personified. How did this character enter the world and work their way into our lives?

Extension/further reading

Ask the children to search for other myth stories from the continent of Africa. African traditions abound with stories that explain how the world is as it is, such as the Benin creation story.

The Hunting of Death

A MYTH FROM RWANDA

The angel huntsmen were close to his heels when Death came to a field, where an old lady was digging.

"Oh glorious, lovely creature!" panted Death. "I have run many miles across this hard world, but never have I seen such a beauty as you! Surely my eyes were made for looking at you. Let me sit here on the ground and gaze at you!"

The old lady giggled. "Ooooh! What a flatterer you are, little crinkly one!"

"Not at all! I'd talk to your father at once and ask to marry you, but a pack of hunters is hard on my heels!"

"I know, I heard God say," said the old woman. "You must be that Death he talked of."

"But *you* wouldn't like me to be killed, would you – a woman of your sweet nature and gentle heart? A maiden as lovely as you would never wish harm on a poor defenceless creature!" The drum beats came closer and closer.

The old woman simpered. "Oh well. Best come on in under here," she said and lifted her skirt, showing a pair of knobbly knee-caps. In out of the sunlight scuttled Death, and twined himself, thin and sinuous, round her legs.

The angel huntsmen came combing the land, the line of them stretching from one horizon to the other. "Have you seen Death pass this way?"

"Not I," answered the old lady, and they passed on, searching the corn ricks, burning the long grass, peering down the wells. Of course, they found no trace of Death.

Out he came from under her skirts, and away he ran without a backward glance. The old woman threw a rock after him, and howled, "Come back! Stop that rascal, God! Don't let him get away! He said he'd marry me!"

But God was angry. "You sheltered Death from me when I hunted him. Now I shan't shelter you from him when he comes hunting for your heartbeat!" And with that he recalled his angel huntsmen to Heaven.

Annotations (left):

simple characterisation:

the lady is old

Death is sly

how Death persuades:

calling her glorious and flattering her

asking her to marry him

calling himself 'poor' and 'defenceless'

God has sent angel huntsmen to pursue Death

like haystacks

Annotations (right):

myths – where the mythic meets the earthly:

mythical figures

a real person

initial capital: Death is a character

alternative words to 'said'

powerful verbs

interesting adjectives

action by a human that will cause problems in the future

5: 2: T1: to identify and classify the features of myths, legends and fables, e.g. the moral in a fable, fantastical beasts in legends

5: 2: T11: to write own versions of legends, myths and fables, using structures and themes identified in reading

Orpheus and Eurydice
retold by Geraldine McCaughrean

Background

The tale of Orpheus is one of the most famous of the Greek myths. Greek myths present a complex world with various gods and beasts inhabiting several domains. In this extract Orpheus, the musician who can tame beasts with a lyre, visits the world of the dead to retrieve his wife, Eurydice. We join Orpheus on a boat trip across the River Styx into the world of the dead, piloted by the ferryman who takes the souls of the dead into the underworld. Orpheus retrieves Eurydice but on the return journey, just as they see the first hint of the sun, he fatally takes one look back to check that it is she who is following him and, as a result, she is lost for ever.

Shared reading and discussing the text

● Myths take place in a universe in which the laws of nature have yet to be formed. As such, we witness gods meeting humans, and people being able to move from this world to the underworld. Ask the children to pick out the locations and characters Orpheus encounters. Map these on the board along a line that begins and ends with the words *River Styx*.

● Myths often show heroes being given challenges that they have to try to overcome. Ask the children to read through the text and pick out the things that present a challenge to Orpheus. There is the fearful dog Cerberus, the cantankerous Pluto (King of the Dead) and then the falling of Eurydice into the darkness. What does Orpheus do to try to tackle these challenges?

● Ask the children to consider other stories in which the heroine or hero has to take a journey into a deadly 'underworld'-like setting and compare them with this extract. Can they find similarities and differences? Entering alone into a place of fear is a common motif, prompting comparison with the stories and films of Harry Potter, Star Wars and James Bond.

● Pick out the commas in the text and examine the functions they are performing. These include marking out an inserted clause, separating clauses in a complex sentence, marking speech and qualifying nouns and verbs.

Activities

● Ask the children to write a short paragraph explaining why the final challenge to Orpheus is so devastating. They may want to consider the way in which it challenges his fear, not for himself, but for Eurydice. There is also the fact that it is such an easy thing to do – that is, just taking one look. They could also reflect on the journey Orpheus has undertaken and how it has been made so difficult by the condition Pluto has imposed upon him.

● Ask the children to create their own underworld into which a character could venture. They will need to plan obstacles and how the character can meet these challenges. What special skills will their character possess? They can also create their own mythical beasts along the way.

● Ask the children to retell this part of the story as a comic strip, deciding which speech they will place into speech bubbles, displaying the communication between characters.

Extension/further reading

Children may be familiar with the Disney cartoon version of the story of Hercules. The closing scenes take up the notion of retrieving a loved one from the underworld. Children could watch this scene and compare it with the Orpheus story.

5: 2: T1: to identify and classify the features of myths, legends and fables, e.g. the moral in a fable, fantastical beasts in legends

5: 2: T2: to investigate different versions of the same story in print or on film, identifying similarities and differences; recognise how stories change over time and differences of culture and place that are expressed in stories

Orpheus and Eurydice

As the boat glided across the river, a dark shape loomed up, then a terrible barking split the air. It was Cerberus, the three-headed guard dog. Orpheus took his lyre on to his lap and began to play. He played a song without words, and the ferryman stopped splashing his oars to listen. The barking sank to a yelp, then to a whimper. When the boat touched shore, Orpheus stepped out of the boat, still playing.

Throughout the Underworld, the souls of the Dead stopped to listen. Pluto, King of the Dead, also listened. "What's that noise, wife?"

His wife, Persephone, knew at once, "It must be Orpheus the musician! Oh, if he is dead and his spirit is ours to keep, we shall have better music here than on earth!"

"Never! Music is forbidden here!" exclaimed Pluto.

At the sight of Orpheus – a man still wearing his earthly body – Pluto jumped up and pointed an angry finger. "You'll be sorry you dared to sneak down here, young man!"

Orpheus simply began to sing. He sang of Eurydice's beauty. He sang of their love. He sang of the spiteful snake and his unbearable loneliness. When the song finished, Pluto sank back into his throne, his hands over his face, and tears running down into his beard.

"Every time someone dies, there are people who want them alive again," said Pluto. "But you are the only one who ever made me allow this to happen. Eurydice shall return to the earth."

He clapped his hands, and feet could be heard running down a long corridor: the footsteps of Eurydice.

Orpheus peered through the gloom for a first glimpse of her dear face.

"If—" said Pluto.

"If?"

"If you can climb back to the sunlight without once turning to look at her face." He laughed unkindly.

Back Orpheus went towards the River Styx, and the swish of a woman's robes followed him. But he did not look back. Again Orpheus began to play. Again the great dog Cerberus lolled with delight and let him pass, licking him with three tongues. But Orpheus did not look back. Into the rowing boat he stepped, and someone stepped in behind him. The ferryman rowed two passengers across the river.

One last long climb and they would be free of the Underworld! Then Orpheus would be able to take Eurydice in his arms and kiss her and laugh about the dreary Kingdom of the Dead. "Not long now!" he called to her.

Why did Eurydice not reply? Perhaps Pluto had tricked him. Perhaps it was someone else following him. Or perhaps Eurydice had changed during her time in the Underworld, and didn't love her husband any more! Just as the first rays of sunlight came into view, Orpheus glanced quickly over his shoulder – just to be sure.

Oh yes, it was Eurydice. Those eyes, that hair, that sweet mouth calling his name: *"Orpheus!"*

She sank down like a drowning swimmer: "Orpheus, why?" She fell back down and the darkness swallowed her up.

"Eurydice!"

But she was gone. Orpheus had lost his beloved a second time.

obstacle on the journey

comma separating phrases (2nd phrase develops the 1st one)

obstacle on the journey

comma separating clauses in a complex sentence

commas demarcating an inserted clause

comma marking phrase that qualifies the noun 'Cerberus'

the central challenge is presented – it may be hard for Orpheus not to be tempted to look back

ways the hero overcomes obstacles

insecurity of Orpheus leads to temptation which causes failure

5: 2: T11: to write own versions of legends, myths and fables, using structures and themes identified in reading

5: 2: S5: to use punctuation effectively to signpost meaning in longer and more complex sentences

Hare, Hippo and Elephant retold by Michael Rosen

Background

In West and Southern Africa there is a wealth of stories from the oral tradition in which the character Hare tricks other animals. Hare is a character who has links with the Brer Rabbit of American folklore. In the story here, Hare is newly married and it should be his job to do the ploughing. But he is averse to hard work and will do anything to avoid it. Then he has an idea. Through undertaking this trick he causes both the Hippo and Elephant to plough up the ground for him.

Shared reading and discussing the text

● Give the children the background to the story, then ask them to look through the text to establish that this is not a true life story. After reading about the trick, what thoughts do they have about the characters? Refer them back to work on characterisation in Term 1 (see pages 10 and 16). Point out that this is a traditional tale that has been told for generations and the details of names (other than Hare, Hippo and Elephant!), character features and setting are left out. Another element is that the plot is simple in structure and easy to remember for oral retelling.

● Trickster stories often contain a conversation in which the trick is hatched (compare this story with that of Till Owlyglass, see page 54). Focus on the conversation between the characters at the beginning of the story and ask the children to gauge their attitudes. Ask them to try saying the words in the manner of the speakers, possibly adding some persuasive or dismissive lines of their own. What attitude does each speaker have and how would his tone of voice reflect it? In the oral transmission of the tale this conversation would provide the teller with a great opportunity to act out the mannerisms and beguiling nature of the seemingly innocent hare. Look at the challenge he presents to the two other animals and ask the children how likely they think it is that he wins the tug of war.

● Repetition, and language that depicts the passing of time, are also common features in oral storytelling. Point out the repeated words in the story, such as *heaved* as the hippo and elephant pull on the rope. Point out how a long period of time is depicted in just two sentences (*The sun went down… The sun came up…*).

● In a shared writing session, ask the children to work in small groups devising a diagram of the story. It should show the structure of the two conversations, the trick involving the two characters Hippo and Elephant and the outcome. Compare the children's diagrams and look for common features. Reproduce the structures on the board or gather items from a few to create a new diagram.

Activities

● Using small rectangles of paper, the children could storyboard the story as if they were making a cartoon. They should imagine every shot or every ten seconds of the film and on each rectangle make a rough sketch of what the viewer can see. A shot could be a close-up on Hare as he speaks, or it could be the elephant who has not yet seen the hippo. Whatever the shot, they should provide a sketch and a note about characters' expressions and words.

● Ask the children to devise their own trickster story about the hare. This should be a traditional tale in which the hare tricks another animal. For example, how could the hare trick another animal into carrying the harvest to a barn or breaking down a wall that he wants demolished? Something to watch when children are using a traditional tale as a stimulus for their own writing is that they keep the tale rooted in its own world – rather than introducing police cars and trips to Los Angeles.

Extension/further reading

Children can look at other stories that anthropomorphise animals and compare the different ways in which it is done, from the animal people of Disney's *Robin Hood* to the animals covertly conversing in *Charlotte's Web*.

Collect other stories about animal tricksters, including the Brer Rabbit stories, for the children to read.

5: 2: T1: to identify and classify the features of myths, legends and fables, e.g. the moral in a fable, fantastical beasts in legends

5: 2: T3: to explore similarities and differences between oral and written storytelling

5: 2: T11: to write own versions of legends, myths and fables, using structures and themes identified in reading

HARE, HIPPO AND ELEPHANT

Hare was a lazy thing and when he got married and settled down he couldn't be bothered to get down to hard work. Go out and work in the fields so he could feed his wife and himself? Not on your life.

Then one day he had an idea. He took a long rope and went into the forest to find Hippo.

"Uncle, will you listen to me a moment? Why don't we have a game here. I tie this rope to you, and I'll see if I can pull you out of the mud."

"Right," said Hippo, "sounds like a great game to me. I can't lose."

"Good," said Hare, "so I'll go off among the trees over there. The moment you feel a tug on the rope, you pull like mad, OK? But I'm warning you, I'm pretty strong."

Hippo laughed. "Yes, of course you are, Hare."

Hare tied the rope round Hippo and then went off among the trees and waited. It wasn't long before Elephant came down to the water-hole.

Hare stopped him. "Oh, uncle, have you got a moment? I'm looking for someone who wants a tug-of-war. Everyone I have a go with, I beat. What do you say?"

"Out of my way, little fool. I haven't got time to play silly games."

"No listen, uncle, I tell you what, if you win, I'll do anything you want.

I'll be your servant, I'll fetch and carry, anything."

Elephant liked the sound of that very much indeed. So he let Hare tie the rope round him and off went Hare, telling Elephant to start pulling when he felt a tug on the rope.

Half-way along the rope where neither Hippo nor Elephant could see him, Hare gave a tug on the rope, first one way and then the other. At once Elephant and Hippo started heaving on the rope. They heaved and they pulled for hours. The sun went down, and they heaved all night. The sun came up again, and still they heaved until they could heave no more and fell down exhausted.

They rested and when they staggered to their feet, both animals wondered just how Hare had managed it and started walking towards each other. When they met, they untied the rope from each other's waists.

"Next time we see Hare, let's kill him," they said.

The next day Hare went out and was rather pleased to see that the ground was all churned up. Just ready to plant my seeds in, he thought, and just think – I didn't even have to do any heavy digging and ploughing. Won't my wife be pleased with me!

---

features indicating this is not a true story – animals who are able to talk and tie ropes

what tone of voice is Hare using? how would you communicate this in storytelling?

Hare presents the challenge – makes reader think about how likely it is that he will win

conversations move the action forwards

characterisation helps us to form images of Hippo and Elephant: attitudes of speakers communicated by speech

repetition is a common feature of traditional tales (helps with oral storytelling as it is important for people to be able to remember the words)

shows the passing of time

specific words used to show how the characters feel

5: 2: S6: to be aware of the differences between spoken and written language, including:
● conventions to guide reader
● the need for writing to make sense away from immediate context
● the use of punctuation to replace intonation, pauses, gestures
● the use of complete sentences

Till Owlyglass

by Michael Rosen

Background

Legends differ from myths in terms of where they are set. A myth takes place in a time outside the laws of nature and a scientifically understood world. While legends may include unnatural events, they nonetheless take place in a 'more real' world. Till Eulenspiegel or Till Owlyglass is a character from German folk legend. He's a scoundrel who tends to cheat and swindle others and manages to get away with it. From his very earliest years right through to his death there are stories of how Till cheated different people.

In this tale Till has arrived at a town of great learning. This extract shows him taking on the professors of the esteemed university. He presents them with the fact that he can perform a great act of education – he is able to teach a donkey to read.

Shared reading and discussing the text

● Read as far as the words *'Let me show you'* and ask the children to predict what trick Till might have up his sleeve. Somehow he will convince the professors that a donkey can read. Record their predictions on the board to revisit once they have read the whole text.

● Read to the end and ask the children to explain the trick Till performed. Can they say how the donkey was reading? Note details such as the letters used and the oats between the pages. Compare this trick with the activity of the hare in 'Hare, Hippo and Elephant' (see page 52). Ask the children to underline similarities. They may notice the boasting of the protagonist and the incredulity of the audience.

● Chart the relationship between Till and the professors. Begin by looking through the passage and picking out things that indicate what the professors are like. Look at how the relationship between Till and the professors changes in the course of the story and mark key stages in this relationship on the text.

● Pick out ten key words that a storyteller could keep as notes to remember the story when retelling it. Focus on the words that Till says and consider the intonation and gestures he would

use. Now do the same for the professors. Storytelling can often involve adding new lines of dialogue. What would the children add if they were retelling the story? Perhaps they would want to add more lines from Till as he leads the professors into the stable.

● Continuing with this scene, encourage the children to imagine how the professors would conduct themselves, as one of them says, *'He can't have done it'*, down to *'The man's an idiot'*. In reality, how much would they interrupt each other? What non-verbal huffs and whistles of incomprehension would they make? Yet in the text we have three, simple, clearly stated lines. Use these for a comparison of the nature of spoken and written language.

Activities

● Ask the children to make notes that will enable them to retell the story. They should aim to summarise each event in one or two words, and each piece of dialogue spoken by Till and the professors with similar brevity. These notes can be written on large sheets of paper to act as cue cards in children's retelling.

● Ask the children to annotate the large cue cards, noting how the characters would have spoken. They will need to consider facial expression and how intonation changes according to meaning, whether it is a scoundrel boasting, professors raising a question or a donkey 'reading a book'.

● Suggest to the children that they create their own Till story – perhaps Till wins a bet, defeats a villain or gets the better of a king. The main focus should be on the way he boasts and the manner in which other characters respond.

Extension/further reading

Why do animals make noises? Why do cows moo? This could be set as a research challenge.

Children could read other stories of Till Owlyglass and search for information about Till Eulenspiegel. Michael Rosen's retelling on audio cassette of *The Wicked Tricks of Till Owlyglass* (BBC Audio) injects a liveliness into the tales.

5: 2: T1: to identify and classify the features of myths, legends and fables, e.g. the moral in a fable, fantastical beasts in legend

5: 2: T3: to explore similarities and differences between oral and written storytelling

5: 2: T11: to write own versions of legends, myths and fables, using structures and themes identified in reading

makes reader wonder what the professors are like

reader predicts:
what could Till be planning?
which letters could he paint?

reader now knows the situation – he will teach a donkey to read

how would these lines be spoken in real life?
how would the feelings of the speakers be communicated?

central point of the legend about Till – the trick he has planned is revealed

Till Owlyglass

Till took the little donkey[K] to the stable of the inn where he was staying and off went the professors,[K] still giggling.[K] They were sure they had fooled Till this time.

Now Till went to the bookbinders[K] and bought a book with no words in it. And afterwards he went back to the inn and on each page of the book he painted[K] some letters. And he sent for the professors again, and back they came.

"He can't have done it," said one.

"No one can teach a donkey to read," said another.

"The man's an idiot,[K]" said a third.

"Gentlemen," said Till, leading the professors into the stable. "My pupil can't read many words yet, but he's made a start. Let me show you."

Till led the donkey up to the book and slipped a few oats[K] between the pages.

The donkey got excited and began to look for the oats, turning the pages of the book. As he turned them, he brayed,[K] "Eee-arr, eee-arr, eee-arr."

And what Till had painted on the pages of the book were the letters[K] E and R.

"Eee-arr, eee-arr, eee-arr!" the donkey went on.

"There," said Till. "He's a bit slow, but he's coming on, the clever little fellow, don't you think? Give me a bit more time and I'll soon have him reading fluently."

The professors did not know where to look, or what to say. So they wrapped their long gowns around themselves and hurried out of the stable. Till had certainly taught them a lesson.

* * *

[K] = key words for storytelling

shows a change in the professors' behaviour and attitude and how their relationship with Till is now different

summing up which shows what Till has done

5: 2: S6: to be aware of the differences between spoken and written language, including:
● conventions to guide reader
● the need for writing to make sense away from immediate context
● the use of punctuation to replace intonation, pauses, gestures
● the use of complete sentences

5: 2: T14: make notes of story outline as preparation for oral storytelling

Sir Galahad

by Marcia Williams

Background

In the Arthurian legends the events surrounding the quest for the Holy Grail, the cup used at the Last Supper, are of crucial importance. The tradition holds that the recovery of the Grail causes the revitalisation of the land in time of need and desolation. Others had searched for the Grail – Sir Lancelot being one famous questing knight – but finding it was deemed to be the task of the knight who could sit in the 'Siege Perilous', a reserved place at the Round Table.

Legends like this tell unreal stories but set them in real and historic times. Characters like King Arthur are shrouded in historic mystery.

Shared reading and discussing the text

● Unlike myths, legends involve historical times and settings in memorable and sometimes fantastic stories. Ask the children to circle the words in this text that refer to another historical period or show it is set in the past (for example *knight, siege, sword*). Looking at the illustrations, can the children say what period of time this story is set in? They don't need to give dates, just a sense of what life would be like in this time, where people would live and the sorts of things they would do.

● Read the speeches made by the two characters in the first picture and the first piece of text (to *could bring to an end*). Ask the children what they think the importance of the Grail and the Siege Perilous is. Explain the origin of the Holy Grail and the Siege Perilous, the seat to be taken by the knight who will find the Grail. Read the text as far as the entrance of the young knight and ask the children what they think this young knight will do. Taking their guesses, read to the end. Return to the words *everyone marvelled*. Why do the children think the other knights had this reaction to this event?

● In shared writing, write the words that could have been said by Arthur and another knight (such as Sir Bors) during these events. Plan where these could be inserted into the storyline.

● Pick out and explore features common to legends – language showing the passing of time, a fantastic story set in a real historical situation, the battle of good against evil and the role of magical powers often held by objects or individuals. At the pinnacle of these is the notion of a quest. Ask the children to look to the quest ahead, the solving of mysteries and the outcomes that await the characters. List the questions that are raised by this passage. Who is the stranger? Can the children hazard guesses? Where have these characters come from?

● Point out the use of commas to embed a clause in a sentence. Read the sentence beginning *The time came when Britain…* without the clause *Merlin told the assembled knights*, then with it. Both make sense, the clause being an insertion that develops more detail in the story.

Activities

● Look at the events of the story from the entry of the ancient man. Ask the children to rewrite sentences from this part of the text, substituting nouns for pronouns. What do they notice about the clarity of the sentences? For example, compare *Then came a young knight…* with *Then he came…*

● Ask the children to imagine the sound effects and voices that would feature in a retelling of this story. Can they list the different sounds that would create the right atmosphere for this legend?

Extension/further reading

Marcia Williams' retelling of the Arthur tales, *King Arthur and the Knights of the Round Table* (Walker Books), is well worth reading.

Children could research the lives of knights and their younger pages in medieval times by looking at books such as Richard Platt's *Castle Diary* (Walker Books).

Kevin Crossley-Holland's excellent *The King Who Was and Will Be* (Orion Children's Books) provides an insight into the background of the Arthur stories.

5: 2: T1: to identify and classify the features of myths, legends and fables, e.g. the moral in a fable, fantastical beasts in legend

SIR GALAHAD

idea of good against evil

gives historical setting

events use the setting to build up atmosphere and mood

what has just happened to the doors? what does that tell us about the ancient man?

object that has magical powers

2 clauses separated by commas; if you remove the clause between the commas, the sentence still makes sense – the commas are used to insert more information

connection to Arthur finding the sword in the stone

Look at my once fertile kingdom, completely barren, and my people dying in droves. What can I do, Merlin?

Only the magical Grail has the power to cure these ills. Even the great Merlin is powerless.

As the years and adventures passed, Knights were killed or died, but always others came to fill their place. But still the Siege Perilous stood empty. The time came when Britain was devastated by famine and plague which, Merlin told the assembled Knights, only the finding of the Grail could bring to an end.

Suddenly, there was a loud banging as a gust of wind slammed shut all the palace doors.

Then, as if from nowhere, an ancient man, dressed in white, appeared in the great hall.

Then came a young knight dressed in red, without sword or shield.

As the court watched in silent wonder, the old man led the Red Knight to the Siege Perilous. There, golden letters began to appear, spelling out the young Knight's name.

SIR GALAHAD THE HIGH PRINCE

As the Knight took his seat, everyone marvelled that one so young should sit there. But King Arthur was delighted to have his Knights of the Round Table complete at last.

I know it's for you, son.

NEVER SHALL MAN TAKE ME HENCE, BUT ONLY HE BY WHOSE SIDE I OUGHT TO HANG, AND HE SHALL BE THE BEST KNIGHT IN THE WORLD.

Sir Lancelot realized with joy that Sir Galahad was his son, born to Princess Elaine. He led young Sir Galahad to the river where he had, that morning, seen a floating stone with a sword buried in it. As Lancelot had hoped, Sir Galahad withdrew the sword with ease. But still his son had no shield.

significance of Siege Perilous – the pure knight who finds the Grail will sit there

what does this indicate about future stories?

5: 2: S9: to secure the use of the comma in embedding clauses within sentences

5: 2: S10: to ensure that, in using pronouns, it is clear to what or to whom they refer

Aesop's Fables *Fables 1 and 2*

Background
Like myths and legends, fables can include unnatural events, often featuring animals that talk. The significant feature of a fable is the moral. A fable tells a story that aims to teach a clear lesson or inspire varied opinions or feelings, such as in tales of courage or those that present moral dilemmas.

Shared reading and discussing the text
● Read through 'Things are not always what they seem', then ask the children to picture the events recounted in the fable. Go through any vocabulary that may be unfamiliar, such as *bolted*. Explain that the author is not only narrating what happened, he is also commenting on the character's actions and the moral.

● Do the same as the above with 'Know your limitations'.

● Point out the features of fables that are displayed in both these texts: a short, simple tale often with animals as characters, the animals being able to speak or think aloud like humans, and the moral at the end (often the purpose of the tale).

● Discuss the children's opinions on the morals of these tales, letting them know that they are free to disagree with them, if they wish. Is it always a good idea not to rush things, so that you are sure things are as they appear (fable 1)?

Are we limited to certain actions or can we aspire beyond them (fable 2)?

Activities
● Suggest that the children write a letter to Aesop, making a case for or against the moral of 'Know your limitations'. They should list their points in note form and then write a letter, explaining their response.

● Can the children think of their own fable to illustrate the moral of 'Things are not always what they seem'? Encourage them to use animals as characters (including their thoughts and speech) and bring out the mistake their main character makes at the end.

● Ask the children to write an alternative fable to 'Know your limitations', with a moral that is at odds with the original (for example, 'You can aspire to do something new'). They can create new characters or retain the original ones.

Extension/further reading
Children can look at other collections of fables from Aesop, for example *Aesop's Funky Fables* by Vivien French (Puffin Books) in which some of them have been rewritten in verse form. *The Hare and the Tortoise and Other Animal Stories* by Sally Grindley (Bloomsbury) presents a set of fables to which extra detail about the characters and settings has been added.

5: 2: T1: to identify and classify the features of myths, legends and fables, e.g. the moral in a fable, fantastical beasts in legends

5: 2: T11: to write own versions of legends, myths and fables, using structures and themes identified in reading

AESOP'S FABLES

THINGS ARE NOT ALWAYS WHAT THEY SEEM

There was a dog which was fond of eating eggs. Mistaking a shell-fish for an egg one day, he opened his mouth wide and bolted it with one great gulp. The weight of it in his stomach caused him intense pain. "Serve me right," he said, "for thinking that anything round must be an egg."

People who rush at things without using judgement run themselves into strange and unexpected dangers.

simple animal character, not much detail given

leads straight into the story

gulp down

narrator comments on moral of story

moral links to the title

is this a good moral? is it unwise to rush into tasks?

KNOW YOUR LIMITATIONS

A man owned a Maltese spaniel and an ass. He made a habit of playing with the dog, and whenever he dined out he used to bring back something to give it when it came and fawned on him. The ass was jealous; and one day it ran up to its master and frisked around him ~ with the result that the master received a kick which made him so angry that he told his servants to drive the ass off with blows and tie it to its manger.

Nature has not endowed us all with the same powers. There are things that some of us cannot do.

features of fables: no detail given about characters; kept simple

was the ass in the wrong?

was the man in the wrong?

narrator comments on moral of story

give/invest

show extreme affection

how did the master receive a kick?

moral of the story

but can't we all try to do what we aspire to do?

features of a fable:

short and simple,

animal characters,

animals speak and think

The Austere Academy
by Lemony Snicket

Background

In this extract, taken from the novel *The Austere Academy*, the three main characters, the Baudelaire orphans, are inducted into Prufrock Academy, a bizarre school. The novel is from *A Series of Unfortunate Events*, a collection of stories that will eventually number 13 books, written by Lemony Snicket. All the books are characterised by a distinctive narrative voice (Snicket being the pseudonym used by the man who passes himself off as the author's 'handler', Daniel Handler). The series tells of the misfortunes that befall the three Baudelaire children. However, Snicket regularly intrudes with oblique references to some terrible events of his own, involving his beloved Beatrice. These are added to by the 'About the author' blurbs in each book, painting an equally bizarre image of the author. Through this text children will be able to appreciate fully the role of the narrator.

Shared reading and discussing the text

● Explain that the *I…* in this passage is a narrator. He is telling the tale of Violet but also slipping in some of his own reflections. Distinguish between the author – who types the words but who has created the narrator – and the narrator, the voice that is telling a story. Point out that an author may pretend to be someone else and adopt a particular narrative voice (whether it is in the first or third person). Look again at the way the narrator makes it sound as if the events took place – an example of the author taking on a narrator's voice.

● Look at the text from *Mr Remora was Violet's teacher…* to the end and ask the children to underline any parts of this section that are the narrator's opinions. Establish that even though the narrator is now telling events in the third person he is still lacing the lines with his point of view (for example, *as if somebody had chopped off a gorilla's thumb*).

● Explore why a passage like this would appeal to children. Can any sections be identified as making you want to read more (for example, the presentation of the teacher)? In this series the narrator's voice is used specifically to draw children in and hold their attention, from the very first book in which readers are warned to discard the novel because it is so terrible.

Activities

● Encourage the children to write their own passage in which they use the *I…* format, as the narrator. Point out that the narrator in this text teasingly gives away a few details of his experience. Can they do the same? They can identify the sort of person they think would read their passage (and the age of their audience) and include some sentences which are directly aimed at the reader (*You…*). Compare these sentences in the children's writing – can they see how they vary depending on the audience to whom they are addressed?

● The reader can infer from the text that there is a separate tale about Beatrice. Can the children create their own story about her? We are only given sketchy details – they could read the first seven books in the series and not find out very much more. If they were in a room with the narrator, what would they ask him? What can they figure out from the triptych that is described in the text?

● Ask the children to adopt distinctive narrative voices in their own paragraphs of writing. For example, can they write in the voice of a fearful and nervous narrator? Or a careless one who doesn't mind what happens to the characters in the tale?

Extension/further reading

Ask the children to look in the school library for other texts in which the narrator inserts his own reflections (using *I…*).

'I' is the narrator, 'you' is the reader

narrator can make up the characters, and narrator himself can be a piece of fiction (he does not exist in real life)

The Austere Academy

If you have walked into a museum recently – whether you did so to attend an art exhibition or to escape from the police – you may have noticed a type of painting known as a triptych. A triptych has three panels, with something different painted on each of the panels. For instance, my friend Professor Reed made a triptych for me, and he painted fire on one panel, a typewriter on another, and the face of a beautiful, intelligent woman on the third. The triptych is entitled *What Happened to Beatrice* and I cannot look upon it without weeping.

I am a writer, and not a painter, but if I were to try and paint a triptych entitled *The Baudelaire Orphans' Miserable Experiences at Prufrock Prep*, I would paint Mr Remora on one panel, Mrs Bass on another, and a box of staples on the third, and the results would make me so sad that between the Beatrice triptych and the Baudelaire triptych I would scarcely stop weeping all day.

Mr Remora was Violet's teacher, and he was so terrible that Violet thought that she'd almost rather stay in the Orphans Shack all morning and eat her meals with her hands tied behind her back rather than hurry to Room One and learn from such a wretched man. Mr Remora had a dark and thick moustache, as if somebody had chopped off a gorilla's thumb and stuck it above Mr Remora's lip, and also like a gorilla, Mr Remora was constantly eating bananas. Bananas are a fairly delicious fruit and contain a healthy amount of potassium, but after watching Mr Remora shove banana after banana into his mouth, dropping banana peels on the floor and smearing banana pulp on his chin and in his moustache, Violet never wanted to see another banana again.

makes us wonder why; leaves unanswered questions

indicates narrator's feelings about events and characters

narrator's opinions communicated directly and by choice of verbs (to denote action)

use of humour in way teacher is presented gives the story popular appeal

5: 2: T8: to distinguish between the author and the narrator, investigating narrative viewpoint and the treatment of different characters, e.g. minor characters, heroes, villains, and perspectives on the action from different characters

5: 2: S3: to understand how writing can be adapted for different audiences and purposes, e.g. by changing vocabulary and sentence structures

Travel

by Edna St Vincent Millay

Background

This classic poem can be used as a starting point for looking at the way a poem can use and develop a particular image (in this case, a train) to encapsulate and explore an emotion. It was this sort of poem that proved controversial for the poet, Edna St Vincent Millay (1892–1950). It was seen as slightly outrageous for a woman to be writing about breaking loose and asserting her freedom.

Shared reading and discussing the text

● Read the poem to the children, then ask them to read through it silently a second time. Can they spot the theme? They will not know until the third stanza that what the poet is expressing is her desire to travel, to escape from the daily grind. The first stanza represents daytime, and the second, night-time. During the day the poet refuses to be distracted by any passing conversations she can hear – what is important to her is the sound of a train in the distance (a symbol of her escape). And at night it is the same – any trains that go by are seen clearly in her mind, even though she should really be asleep. Establish that it doesn't really matter whether there are actually any trains or not – it may be that she is imagining them – it is the feelings of the poet that are behind the true meaning of the poem.

● The train and track provide an image – but what do they represent? Help the children to see how they signify the poet's longing to get away and contribute to the feelings expressed by the line *Though the night is still for sleep and dreaming* and the last stanza.

● Pick out the way in which the words *but* and *yet* are used in the three stanzas, enabling the poet to make contrasts, for example *My heart is warm with the friends I make… Yet there isn't a train…* – the second two lines of the stanza being opposed to the first two lines.

● Look at the rhyme scheme of the poem. In each stanza, circle the line endings that rhyme

with each other. Children should see a structure emerging. Now re-read the poem, asking the children to listen to the rhymes.

Activities

● Children can write their own three paragraphs in which they focus on the travels they would wish to undertake in later life. They can think of specific places and add details of what they would hope to see and experience in such locations. Or they could adopt a more generalised approach and write about the types of places they would like to visit.

● Ask the children to use the structure of this poem to attempt their own rhymed lines. They can use the thought of travel – and where they would one day like to go – as inspiration. Using the -*ing* verb ending, they could create two new lines and separate these with a new first and third line, following the structure of the poem.

● Ask the children to annotate a photocopy of the poem, circling the ten most memorable words in the text and making brief notes on why each matters so much. These can be evocative adjectives, powerful verbs or names of things that are central to the idea of the poem.

Extension/further reading

Writing about travel plans can be linked to map work, with children developing their map skills and use of atlases and writing about the route they would most like to take.

Films or stories that tap into children's sense of adventure and tie in with this text, such as Edith Nesbit's *The Railway Children* (Puffin Books), could be used as a basis for extension work.

Encourage the children to find further poems which feature trains – there is 'Adelstrop' by Edward Thomas and 'Night Mail' by WH Auden, for example. Both can be found in the anthology *I Like This Poem* edited by Kaye Webb (Puffin Books). Explore the poems' meaning, and add them to a class anthology.

5: 2: T12: to use the structures of poems read to write extensions based on these, e.g. additional verses, or substituting own words and ideas

5: 2: T7: to compile a class anthology of favourite poems with commentaries which illuminate the choice

the title simplifies what the poem is about, but doesn't give any clues about the thoughts and feelings of the poet

connects to the theme of the poem – life for the poet has a dreamlike quality to it as she focuses on her longing to travel

explains that she would rather leave those friends if it means that she can travel

Travel

The railroad track is miles away, [1]
    And the day is loud with voices speaking, [2]
Yet there isn't a train goes by all day [3]
    But I hear its whistle shrieking. [4]

All night there isn't a train goes by, [5]
    Though the night is still for sleeping and dreaming, [6]
But I see its cinders red on the sky, [7]
    And hear its engine steaming. [8]

My heart is warm with the friends I make, [9]
    And better friends I'll not be knowing, [10]
Yet there isn't a train I wouldn't take, [11]
    No matter where it's going. [12]

Edna St Vincent Millay

lines 1 and 3 rhyme

lines 2, 4, 6, 8, 10 and 12 are connected as rhymes by 'ing' endings

lines 5 and 7 rhyme

lines 9 and 11 rhyme

theme of the poem – the poet's longing to go away – expressed in the last 2 lines

this is like the 'but' in the 2nd stanza – it is used to add something more that contrasts with what has just been said

the poet says that she could never have better friends than the ones she has now

An Elegy on the Death of a Mad Dog

by Oliver Goldsmith

Background

Written in 1766, Goldsmith's elegiac poem applies a witty twist to the idea of a poem being about the mourning for a person or a lament for something tragic that has happened. It overturns what the reader is expecting – that the mad dog will poison the good man – and leaves the mad dog dying. Goldsmith (1728–1774) was the author of, among other works, *The Vicar of Wakefield* and *She Stoops to Conquer*. He was a harsh critic of sentimental attitudes and social custom. In his time it would indeed not have been uncommon to find an elegy or ballad about a dear old man who sadly dies, having been bitten by a wicked dog. This poem turns that sort of sentimentalism on its head.

Shared reading and discussing the text

● Explain to the children that an elegy is a poem that is a lament, often for someone who has died. Read as far as the end of the seventh stanza, then ask the children to consider what they think will happen in the last stanza. They should bear in mind what the poem has said about people's reactions to the event. Why do the people expect the man to die? Now read the last stanza. Ask the children what we are now to make of the man.

● Having read the poem, explore what has happened in it. Ask the children to look carefully at the second and third stanzas to find out what everyone thought of the man. Encourage them to provide you with a one-sentence answer, supporting it with words from the poem. Moving on to the fourth stanza, can they see how the dog is shown in contrast to the man? What would they make of a dog that bit such a man? How would the dog have known this was *so good a man* (stanza 6)? But there is a twist in this tale – it is the dog who dies. Can the children think of reasons for this? Perhaps the man has poison in him that has been transmitted to the dog. How does the ending change the reader's thoughts about the man and the dog?

● Make a list of the unfamiliar words in the poem (for example, *wondrous, whelp, pique*). Ask the children to attempt to define them from the context, and work with them to annotate the text. Allow them to suggest various definitions, encouraging them to justify those they offer. Once these have been provided, resort to a dictionary for further clarification.

● Look at the word order within the poem. The poetic nature of the sentences guides the word order – *It was the dog that died* is reordered for effect. Ask the children to look through the poem for sentences that they could say in a different way, reordering the words (for example, *There was a man in Islington*).

● Pick out the rhyme structure and make a list of the rhyming words in the poem (*sort, short; song, long* and so on).

Activities

● There are eight stanzas in the poem. Ask the children to illustrate each one and make a comic strip version of the poem by cutting out the stanzas individually, placing them underneath the relevant pictures and adding speech and thought bubbles. They can then paste everything into position on a large sheet of paper.

● Ask the children to write a short dialogue between two of the neighbours. What might they have said to each other? They will need to think through everything the neighbours would have seen (and what they would have expected) and the surprise they would have felt when things turned out the way they did.

● Can the children create their own stanza for Goldsmith's 18th-century poem? Perhaps the man who was bitten by the dog encounters a rat, and the rat comments on the dog's death. They should follow the rhyme structure of Goldsmith's original and create a word order which is similar in style.

Extension/further reading

Ask the children to find images that show London during the 18th century. This will help them to visualise what life was like at the time Goldsmith was writing.

5: 2: T4: to read a range of narrative poems

5: 2: T6: to understand terms which describe different kinds of poems, e.g. *ballad, sonnet, rap, elegy, narrative poem,* and to identify typical features

5: 2: T12: to use the structures of poems read to write extensions based on these, e.g. additional verses, or substituting own words and ideas

a lament (expressing grief) for the dead

complex order of words, but means that the poem need not hold the reader's attention for too long

perceived qualities of the man – what others think he is like

2 stanzas present a contrast between the man and dog

poem has unfamiliar words, which tell us it was written a long time ago

how would the dog have known that the man was good?
what did the neighbours expect? (that so good a man would be protected)

provides a twist in the tale

An Elegy on the Death of a Mad Dog

Good people all, of every sort,
    Give ear unto my song;
And if you find it wondrous short,
    It cannot hold you long.

In Islington there was a man,
    Of whom the world might say,
That still a godly race he ran,
    Whene'er he went to pray.

A kind and gentle heart he had,
    To comfort friends and foes;
The naked every day he clad,
    When he put on his clothes.

And in that town a dog was found,
    As many dogs there be,
Both mongrel, puppy, whelp, and hound,
    And curs of low degree.

This dog and man at first were friends;
    But when a pique began,
The dog, to gain his private ends,
    Went mad, and bit the man.

Around from all the neighbouring streets
    The wondering neighbours ran,
And swore the dog had lost his wits,
    To bite so good a man.

The wound it seemed both sore and sad
    To every Christian eye;
And while they swore the dog was mad,
    They swore the man would die.

But soon a wonder came to light,[1]
    That showed the rogues they lied:[2]
The man recovered of the bite,[3]
    The dog it was that died.[4]

Oliver Goldsmith

wonderfully

pleasing to God

aggressive dogs

argument

senses

same rhyme structure for each stanza:

1st and 3rd lines rhyme

2nd and 4th lines rhyme

5: 2: S1: to re-order simple sentences, noting the changes which are required in word order and verb forms and discuss the effects of changes

5: 2: S8: to construct sentences in different ways, while retaining meaning, through:
● combining two or more sentences
● re-ordering them
● deleting or substituting words
● writing them in more telegraphic ways

Journey of the Magi

by TS Eliot

Background

Last century, TS Eliot was one of the greatest writers in the English language. His longer poems require a fair amount of fathoming. This shorter narrative poem gives an insight into some of the features that made his work so great. Here we have an excellent theme, strong, clear voices in the poem and lots of references to another texts – in this case, the Christian Gospel. This poem is inspired by the story of the three wise men (the Magi) who visited the infant Jesus, as told in Matthew 2: 1–12.

Shared reading and discussing the text

● Explain the title to the children – who the Magi were, for example. What journey do the children think they are going on?

● Ask the children to read the poem up to the word *satisfactory* at the end of the second stanza. Can they pick out the parts of the narrative that show the various experiences that the Magi had along the way? Ask them to list the features that made it *A hard time* (line 16) – the bad treatment the travellers received, for example. A turning point comes when they descend to the temperate valley. Explain that *temperate* means 'mild'.

● Read through the whole poem. Ask for the children's initial responses to the final stanza. After all the twists and turns of the journey what is the narrator saying about how the journey ended? Point out that this is a tough text and all suggestions are worth voicing as there isn't one final explanation of this (or any) poem.

● The poem is narrated by one of the Magi. Take the opportunity to point out the difference between the author (TS Eliot) and the narrator. Listening to this narrative voice retelling the journey, how do the children think he feels about the visit he made all those years ago and what he experienced? Begin by looking at the first half of the poem, already visited above, then return to the final lines of the poem. In what way was their journey like a death? What birth was involved? What do they think of the declaration that *it was (you may say) satisfactory*?

● Ask the children to pinpoint some of the images used in the poem, for example *The ways deep and the weather sharp* (line 4) and a *running stream and a water-mill beating the darkness* (line 23). What makes them interesting? Weather can be sharp, but how can ways be deep? Encourage them to help you to list other features that are puzzling, such as the white horse and the wine-skins

● Re-read the last section of the poem. *We* turns to *I* as the narrator gets more personal. Talk about the concepts of birth and death that feature in the Christian Gospel (the birth and crucifixion of Jesus, for example). Point out how the journey of the Magi was like death. Try to explain why the narrator would welcome undertaking another similar experience.

Activities

● Ask the children to think of their own journey poem, drawing on this narrative structure. They can write about the trials of a journey. What challenges will they encounter? They should try to let their writing lead up to a moment of reflection, as in Eliot's poem: *but set down this…* They could draw upon the journey of Orpheus (see page 50) or Ruskin Splinter (see page 14). Alternatively, they could draw upon other stories with which they have become familiar in RE lessons.

● Ask the children to research some of the allusions to other features of the Christian story. They could look at the three trees (Luke 23: 32–3), the pieces of silver and the throwing of dice (Matthew 26: 14–15, Matthew 27: 35), the wine-skins (Luke 5: 37–8) and the vine leaves (John 15: 5).

Extension/further reading

Reviewing the stories they have encountered in RE lessons, the children could look for other examples of those who have endured hardships as a part of their faith journey. These could include ancient teachers or modern leaders, such as Ghandi and Martin Luther King. How does this poem reflect something of that experience?

5: 2: T4: to read a range of narrative poems

5: 2: T6: to understand terms which describe different kinds of poems, e.g. *ballad, sonnet, rap, elegy, narrative poem*, and to identify typical features

5: 2: T10: to understand the differences between literal and figurative language, e.g. through discussing the effects of imagery in poetry and prose

the three wise men who visit the infant Jesus

Journey of the Magi

"A cold coming we had of it,
Just the worst time of the year
For a journey, and such a long journey:
The ways deep and the weather sharp,
The very dead of winter."
And the camels galled, sore-footed, refractory,
Lying down in the melting snow.
There were times we regretted
The summer palaces on slopes, the terraces,
And the silken girls bringing sherbet.
Then the camel men cursing and grumbling
And running away, and wanting their liquor and women,
And the night-fires going out, and the lack of shelters,
And the cities hostile and the towns unfriendly
And the villages dirty and charging high prices:
A hard time we had of it.
And the end we preferred to travel all night,
Sleeping in snatches
With the voices singing in our ears, saying
That this was all folly.

Then at dawn we came down to a temperate valley,
Wet, below the snow line, smelling of vegetation,
With a running stream and a water-mill beating the
    darkness,
And three trees on the low sky.
And an old white horse galloped away in the meadow.
Then we came to a tavern with vine-leaves over the lintel,
Six hands at an open door dicing for pieces of silver,
And feet kicking the empty wine-skins.
But there was no information, so we continued
And arrived at evening, not a moment too soon
Finding the place; it was (you may say) satisfactory.

All this was a long time ago, I remember,
And I would do it again, but set down
This set down
This: were we led all that way for
Birth or Death? There was a Birth, certainly,
We had evidence and no doubt. I had seen birth and
    death,
But had thought they were different; this Birth was
Hard and bitter agony for us, like Death, our death.
We returned to our places, these Kingdoms,
But no longer at ease here, in the old dispensation,
With an alien people clutching their gods.
I should be glad of another death.

TS Eliot

narrative voice – 1st person

poem indicates what happened on this journey

language that describes people and places

this was better than staying somewhere for the night and being treated badly

the three crosses of Calvary

inn

understatement – not the climax the reader expects, and nothing is said about the place

absence of comma in between words makes it more difficult to make sense of the text

confusion between birth and death

with sores on their skin

stubborn

a little at a time

foolish – a mistake

a symbol of the darkness receding

throwing dice

top of the door

biblical imagery

used in biblical times for storing wine

'we' turns to 'I' to signify deeper, personal thought

the old religious system, the old way of doing things

why would a person welcome another?

5: 2: T8: to distinguish between the author and the narrator, investigating narrative viewpoint and the treatment of different characters, e.g. minor characters, heroes, villains, and perspectives on the action from different characters

Fairy Tale

by Miroslav Holub

Background

'Fairy Tale' is a short and interesting example of narrative poetry. In this poem a character is portrayed embarking on a strange journey. At the end of the poem we are left wondering where he has gone and what he will do, but children will warm to the way this text opens up the possibility of an adventurous vista.

Shared reading and discussing the text

● Remind the children that a narrative poem is a poem that tells a story. The character in this poem builds and makes a collection of things and then takes his journey into the world. Read the poem and ask the children why they think the text is called 'Fairy Tale'. Suggestions might include the fact that a lot of fairy tales include a journey or that his actions in the last three stanzas appear magical. Ask the children to think about how fairy tales often end. Is this a 'happy ever after' ending? Opinions may vary on this point.

● Ask the children to read through the poem twice, and try to remember as much as they can. Then, hiding the text, ask them to list what the character in the poem did. Make notes about the various actions, images and feelings the children recall from the poem, and what came first, next and so on. Develop their understanding of the narrative of the poem by asking them if they can recall what happened at the end.

● Ask the children what they think happened in the last three stanzas of the poem (from *He cut out his bit of sky above*). These stanzas contain a wealth of imagery – how do the children interpret the cutting out of sky, the wrapping up of items and the lonesomeness of an arctic fox? Distinguish literal from figurative language by focusing on the line *He cut out his...* – both as an image and for what it expresses. Ask the children to imagine someone cutting out sky.

Then ask them what sort of feeling it conjures up – how does it express the way a character cuts out his space in the world or his sense of who he is? Remind them of the poem 'Travel' (see page 62) – another journey poem – in which an interest in trains is used to express a much deeper feeling. Can they apply a similar idea to these stanzas, as the character cuts out his place, his identity, then sets off into the world?

● What do we know about the *he...* in this poem? Look at the various ways in which the character is referred to and circle these. *He* and *his* are used without explaining who *he* is. Exploring narrative viewpoint, explain that this is a narrative poem but the poet is narrating about someone else. What does this do to our understanding of the character and appreciation of his actions? How do the children feel about the character in the poem? And what do they think the narrator's opinion of the character in this poem would be? List the questions they would like to put to the narrator who tells this fairy tale.

Activities

● Ask the children to think of their own poem in the style of 'Fairy Tale' and in which someone takes various things and sets out on a journey. Point out the use of the comma to signpost the list in the poem, encouraging the children to do the same in their own version. They don't have to write a fairy tale, theirs could simply be about a character who sets out on an adventure or a voyage of discovery.

● Switch the poem to the first person and ask the children to pick a few lines from the poem to extend it. Explain that they can use words and images from the poem. Encourage them to leave the poem with an open ending, as it is here.

5: 2: T4: to read a range of narrative poems

5: 2: T6: to understand terms which describe different kinds of poems, e.g. *ballad, sonnet, rap, elegy, narrative poem*, and to identify typical features

5: 2: T10: to understand the differences between literal and figurative language, e.g. through discussing the effects of imagery in poetry and prose

title evokes responses based on other reading experiences

use of commas to demarcate listed items

Fairy Tale

(He) (built) himself a house,
　(his) foundations,
　his stones,
　his walls,
　his roof overhead,
　his chimney and smoke,
　his view from the window.

He (made) himself a garden,
　his fence,
　his thyme,
　his earthworm,
　his evening dew.

He cut out his bit of sky above.

And he (wrapped) the garden in the sky
and the house in the garden
and (packed) the lot in a handkerchief

and went off
lone as an arctic fox
through the cold
unending
rain
into the world.

Miroslav Holub

noun–pronoun agreement

verbs for actions of the central character

feature of narrative poetry – events usually follow each other in chronological order

imagery – conjures up image of character carving out his space in the world

metaphor – dealing with one thing (sky) in language associated with another (material)

simile – likening one thing to another (man to fox) through a similarity (loneliness)

5: 2: S4: to revise from Y4:
● the different kinds of noun
● the function of pronouns
● agreement between nouns, pronouns and verbs

5: 2: S5: to use punctuation effectively to signpost meaning in longer and more complex sentences

Sir Gawain

by Kevin Crossley-Holland

Background

A report text can be thought of as a written snapshot of its subject matter. For this text it would be helpful if children are familiar with the story of Sir Gawain and the Green Knight. And it can be used to make links with the text about Sir Galahad (see page 56). The Sir Galahad text recounts a story about a character; this text meets the requirements of a report by presenting a subject. It includes details about Gawain, explaining his exploits and giving a summation of his character, and mentions the historical evidence of his existence.

Shared reading and discussing the text

● Read through the text and revise the main features of a report text from Year 3 Term 1 and Year 4 Term 1. Point out the general presentation with which the report opens, introducing Arthur's nephew followed by the particular detail in the following paragraphs. Ask the children to go through the text, picking out three specific details which are very different from one another. Can they see any structuring of details into separate sections of the text?

● Explain any difficult phrases and sentences, for example *Medieval romances stretched Gawain's character in opposite directions*. Can the children see that this sentence is describing the way in which Gawain has been portrayed as both a 'good' and 'bad' character, with writers having differing points of view?

● Revise the use of the present tense in reports by finding examples of present tense verbs in this text. Ask the children to say some of these sentences aloud and consider why the text is written in this way. Why should something about the past be written using present tense verbs? Establish that the report text is using the present tense for presenting the current picture of Gawain (for example, *what makes him especially appealing…*), but is also looking back to the past and using the past tense for stating facts (*Gawain was one of the most important knights…*). Read

through the text, finding the sentences that switch to the past tense. Make a list, in note form, of what we are told about what Gawain did (*he rode a horse called Gringalet*, and so on).

● Look at the text closely together and ask the children to find sentences in which there are two clauses. Examples include the second sentence in which the phrases *This was the relationship between King Arthur and Sir Gawain* and *who was the son…* set up two units that could easily be turned into independent sentences but are joined into one, separated only by a comma. Reading on, show the children how the words *and yet* (lines 6/7) place the two surrounding clauses in apposition. Find other examples of complex sentences in the text.

Activities

● This text provides a useful model for children writing a present tense report about the way a particular character is presented in several different tales. Ask the children to think of a character who appears in a number of stories (for example, a cartoon character in a current series) and write a report text about what the character is like, the sorts of things he or she does, and what they think about the character.

● Ask the children to write about this text and the story about Sir Galahad (see page 56), noting what they think they gain from each text. What does the story give that a report can't – and vice versa? Ask the children to write a short paragraph on each, rounding off with a consideration of what sort of text they prefer to read.

Extension/further reading

Look at other legends told in England in the Middle Ages and earlier. Children could explore the lives of invaders and settlers, or the lives of legendary characters such as Robin Hood. There may also be local legends they can draw upon for their own report text on legendary characters.

5: 2: S8: to construct sentences in different ways, while retaining meaning, through:
● combining two or more sentences
● re-ordering them
● deleting or substituting words
● writing them in more telegraphic ways

5: 2: T22: to plan, compose, edit and refine short non-chronological reports and explanatory texts, using reading as a source, focusing on clarity, conciseness, and impersonal style

5: 2: T19: to evaluate texts critically by comparing how different sources treat the same information

2 clauses, each containing a verb ('was') and separated by a comma and the word 'who'

explores a complex subject: his bravery, his humanity or (possibly) his wickedness

clause inserted into a sentence to add more information

sentence makes reader think about the meaning (how can you stretch a character?)

2 verbs, 2 clauses; 'and yet' connects them

verbs in present tense, but past tense also used to recount details relevant to the report

SIR GAWAIN

¹ In the Middle Ages, particularly strong ties linked a man and his sister's son. This was the relationship between King Arthur and Sir Gawain, who was the son of Arthur's sister, Morgause, and King Lot of Orkney.

² Medieval romances stretched Gawain's character in opposite directions. In the wonderful English poem known as *Sir Gawain and the Green Knight*, Gawain is an absolute model of bravery and courtesy, and yet what makes him especially appealing is that he is not quite perfect. He allows himself to be tempted by the beautiful wife of his host. He is a human being! Some French writers, though, show Gawain in a very different light – cheating, disloyal, bitter and violent. But on these points, ³ everyone agrees: Gawain was one of the most important of Arthur's knights. Like the sun, he grew stronger hour by hour until noon, and then weaker hour by hour after noon; he rode a horse called Gringalet; and his terrible feud with his dearest friend, Sir Lancelot, who accidentally killed Gawain's brothers Gareth and Gaheris while saving Queen Guinevere from burning, was a mortal blow to the fellowship of the Round Table.

⁴ In 1485, the printer William Caxton listed the evidence which proved (he said) the existence of King Arthur and his fellowship: the king's tomb at Glastonbury, the Round Table at Winchester, the king's red wax seal at Westminster, Sir Lancelot's sword (he doesn't say where!) – and in Dover Castle, Sir Gawain's skull.

elements of a report text:

1. introduction to subject

2. the two sides of his character

3. his actions

4. the evidence of Caxton

different sections elaborate by giving further details

sections 2 and 3 encourage the reader to make up their own mind about how Sir Gawain is being presented in this text – positively, negatively or a bit of both

The Sun

Background

This report text presents facts about the Sun, and can be viewed in contrast to the explanatory text, 'The Stars' (see page 76), in which similar subject matter is treated in a different way for a different purpose. The report text here presents things as they are; the explanatory text explains a process (the life of a star). This text provides the opportunity for children to examine several significant features of a report, such as the use of technical vocabulary and organising of information.

Shared reading and discussing the text

● Read through the text and mark it up in a way that shows how the report is structured: a general introduction followed by paragraphs that package information into manageable chunks, with specific facts in sub-sections (so that there is a shift from the general to the specific).

● Look through the text and identify the task performed by each of the paragraphs. Annotate the passage with notes that act as a sub-heading for each paragraph or section of text (*what the Sun is, how it links to Earth*, and so on).

● Ask the children to find technical terms in the text (for example *energy, sunspot cycle*). Re-read the text, circling such terms. How many of them are defined in the text (for example *prominences*) and how many are readers expected to know already (for example *helium*)?

● Revise the use of the present tense and read through the text, locating examples of sentences written in the present. Look at the section on features of the Sun and ask the children to imagine they are living on another planet a billion years in the future and writing about the Sun in the past tense. Ask them to rewrite the sentences so that they are in the past tense.

● Can the children suggest what they think are the seven most significant facts listed in the text? Having done this, ask them to think of other ways in which each of these facts could have been incorporated into a sentence.

Activities

● One vital feature of report texts is the way in which pronouns provide cohesion. For example, the word *This* in the third sentence refers to the process described in the second; the word *it* in the fifth continues the reference to the Sun in the fourth. Ask the children to look through the text to find other pronouns, circling them and noting down what they refer to (for example, *This = hydrogen being turned to helium*).

● Challenge the children to use the text to produce their own report. They should first make a list of 30 key words from the text, then at a later date re-read their notes and attempt to use them to write their own report about the Sun.

Extension/further reading

Ask the children to generate questions that could be answered by this text. They could try setting a quiz, devising ten questions – five for each team. Are there any questions about the Sun that the text doesn't answer thoroughly? These could provide a basis for some further research.

5: 2: T20: notemaking: to discuss what is meant by 'in your own words' and when it is appropriate to copy, quote and adapt

5: 2: T22: to plan, compose, edit and refine short non-chronological reports and explanatory texts, using reading as a source, focusing on clarity, conciseness, and impersonal style

general introduction

information gathered in paragraphs:
1. what the Sun is
2. its link to Earth

technical terminology

simple present tense verbs: text records how things are

exploring things that would occur if…

report text begins with the general, then branches into more detail

bullet points to mark out separate sections

units of measurement

specific facts placed in a sub-section

The Sun

1 The Sun, like all stars, is a ball of fiercely **hot gas**. Hydrogen gas deep inside it is constantly being turned into helium. This releases energy in the form of **light** and **heat**.

2 The Sun is the nearest star to Earth. In Space terms it is relatively close – only about 150 million km away! The Sun has shone steadily for thousands of millions of years. If it went dim for only a few days, most life forms on Earth would perish.

Features of the Sun
These are some of the Sun's more **spectacular features**:

● Enormous eruptions of gas, called prominences, rise continually from the surface of the Sun. Some reach out into Space as far as 2 million km.

Arched prominences

Sunspots

● Sunspots are darker, cooler areas that appear on the Sun's surface from time to time. Some are much larger than the Earth and can last for months. Smaller ones last for only a few days or weeks.

● Every 11 years or so, sunspots become more common and then fade away. This is called the sunspot cycle.

Sun facts
● The diameter or distance through the centre of the Sun is 1,392,000km.

● The temperature at the core is believed to be about 14 million °C. At the surface it is 6000°C.

Solar flares
● Solar flares are violent explosions of energy from the Sun's surface. They shoot particles at high speed out into Space. On Earth they can produce strange effects, such as the glowing lights, called aurorae, that sometimes appear in the night sky.

5: 2: W9: to search for, collect, define and spell technical words derived from work in other subjects

5: 2: S4: to revise from Y4:
● the different kinds of noun
● the function of pronouns
● agreement between nouns, pronouns and verbs

The path that's not a promenade

Background

This report text has been taken from a travel section of a newspaper. It focuses on one of the finest (but challenging) coastal paths in Britain, the Pembrokeshire path.

Shared reading and discussing the text

● Explain to the children that travel supplements and articles in newspapers and magazines encourage potential travellers to think about the possibility of visiting a destination and give some advice on what to do and where to go when they get there. Read through the text and mark the features of a report text – for example, general introduction, paragraphs breaking the subject matter down, present tense verbs. Note how further information is provided with the inclusion of particular geographical features, and comments from other people.

● Re-read the text and look for complex sentences in which the clauses are separated by commas. Ask the children to pinpoint the verbs in the text, noting where there is a verb in a clause on one side of a comma and a verb in a clause on the other side.

● Most of the sentences in the passage are in the present tense. Pick out some of them, reading them aloud. Ask the children to try saying the sentences as if they were written in the past tense (for example, *It was not clear how many… The reward was a rich…*).

Activities

● Ask the children to read through the text and, as they read it, make a note of the good points made about the coastal path, for example *spectacular clifftops*. Now read the text slowly and ask the children to check their notes, making further notes, if necessary, during the reading. Remove the text from sight and ask the children to refer to their notes as a means of listing the good points made about the coastal path. They should add their own words, so that their sentences make sense.

● Do the children feel that they would walk along the coastal path themselves? Look at the text again, asking them to think about the good points they have just identified but balancing these against the challenges. How do they think most readers would react to this text? Ask them to list the negative or challenging points raised about the coastal path. What do the quotations add to our perception of this cliff path? Establish that they provide the reader with the 'reality' view.

● Using a copy of the text and working in pairs, the children could underline facts in one colour and opinions in another. Encourage them to compare their outcomes with other pairs to see if they reached a similar agreement about fact and opinion. Explain that they should mark any parts of the text they found difficult to classify.

● This text is accompanied by a map. Provide the children with a local map that shows the location of their school and ask them to plan a route that takes in local sights and places of beauty or interest. Once they have created their route, they should write their own travel piece reporting on the location.

Extension/further reading

Ask the children to watch a holiday programme on the television, making notes on a section of it about a particular location. They can then collate their information and write a non-chronological report about the location.

Alternatively, they could use geography texts to write non-chronological reports about selected locations. They could also look for travel reports in newspapers and on the Internet to see how the features of this type of report are similar across a range of texts.

5: 2: T20: notemaking: to discuss what is meant by 'in your own words' and when it is appropriate to copy, quote and adapt

5: 2: T22: to plan, compose, edit and refine short non-chronological reports and explanatory texts, using reading as a source, focusing on clarity, conciseness, and impersonal style

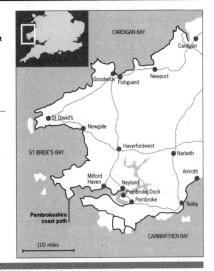

general introductory sentence

use of 2 dashes to add extra information

comparison made with another place

one of the interesting facts inserted into the report

paragraphing to gather the material into chunks

comma to separate clauses in a complex sentence

pros (good points) and cons (bad points) – report text gives an overview of the subject

quotes bring insights from other sources

opinion

verbs in each clause

commas to show embedded clause (a clause within other clauses)

fact

use of present tense

Wind scale... according to Humphrys, a good 10–12 miles' walk with a "really strong wind beating against you is the most energising and wonderful sensation". The Pembrokeshire Coast Path is a challenging hike even for hardened walkers, but offers spectacular rewards such as the view over Marloes Sands

The path that's not a promenade

Anyone walking the full length of the Pembrokeshire Coast Path is certain to end up with a deep tan – from the wind, if not the sun – and calf muscles like Popeye.

The route covers 186 winding, undulating miles –100 of them on spectacular clifftops – and a total ascent and descent of 35,000ft, which is a bit like climbing Everest. The terrain is so rough that when the path was made in the 1960s, they used a small bulldozer to cut through the gorse and blackthorn that cling to the slopes. Even a hardened walker will need 10 days or more to get from Cardigan at the northern end to Amroth in the south.

It's not clear how many people do the whole thing, but about 150 a year are serious enough to register at checkpoints and get a signed certificate from the Pembrokeshire Coast National Park Authority. A recent survey showed that 300,000 people a year set foot on the path and 12,000 cover "a significant distance".

The reward is a rich diet of 500ft cliffs, crashing surf, seal-covered rocks, smugglers' coves, gleaming beaches and multiple relics of the early Celtic church. The only blots are the refineries of Milford Haven and Pembroke power station, but you can dodge these by bus.

Anthony Richards, access officer for the national park authority, says the most popular part is round the cathedral town of St David's and the westernmost tip of Wales. His nominations for best cliff, best beach and best fishing village are Stackpole Head on the southern section, Marloes Sands, and Porth-gain, between Fishguard and St David's.

"I must stress the challenging nature of this path," he says. "It's not a promenade, it's a mountain along a coast. We can give advice about the gentler sections, and there are some places accessible by wheelchair. The path is safe, but not the coast itself."

Every spring, when the coastal flowers are at their best, the authority organises a guided walk along the entire route, with naturalists, ornithologists, archaeologists and geologists. It costs £120, excluding accommodation, and this year runs from May 27 to June 9.

Guides to transport and accommodation along the path are published by the Pembrokeshire Coast National Park Authority, Winch Lane, Haverfordwest SA61 1PY, tel 01437 764636, or visit www.pembrokeshirecoast.org.uk

5: 2: S5: to use punctuation effectively to signpost meaning in longer and more complex sentences

5: 2: S9: to secure the use of the comma in embedding clauses within sentences

The Stars

Background

An explanatory text shows how a process works. In this case it is the life process of a star, an explanatory text within a report text which gives general information about stars. Unlike a recount, which is usually about a specific event, this text refers to any star – that is, the life cycle is common to all stars. The vital feature in this explanation is the passage of time.

Shared reading and discussing the text

● Before reading the text, ask the children what they know about stars. They will probably be aware that the Sun is a star. Ask them to speculate on what happens when a star is first originated and how a star ends. Make notes of their ideas on the board. Ask them to think about the birth and death of stars and come up with some questions about this process. Make a list of the five questions the class agree to be the most pressing. Prompt the use of the words *How* and *Why* at the start of the questions.

● Now read the text. Look back at the list and see which of the children's questions have been answered by the text and what answers have been given. Which processes have been explained?

● Point out the vocabulary used to indicate the passage of time in this text. Which words signal another stage in the process (for example, *As… Eventually…*)?

● Read this text alongside the text on the Sun (see page 72) and ask the children to pick out the different features of structure and language, with a view towards noting the ways in which such texts can be framed. Particularly important features of most explanation texts include a general statement to introduce the topic, a series of logical steps (usually with diagrams), the use of the present tense and temporal (*then, next*) and/or causal (*because, due to*) connectives.

Activities

● Try the five question task with other non-fiction subjects. Ask the children to locate a double-page spread on a subject within a non-fiction text and, without reading the text, list five questions about the subject concerned. They should then read the text to find any answers. Encourage them to carry out some research to resolve the unanswered questions.

● Ask the children to read through the text and locate any words that are subject specific, such as *supernova* and *white dwarf*, and circle them. Can they write a short glossary, compiling a list of such terms?

● Ask the children to use the information presented in the text to create a large poster that could teach this subject matter to children in Year 4 (Primary 5). Remind them to take notes from the text, rather than copying it out in full.

Extension/further reading

Encourage the children to look for the structure of report and explanatory texts in other science texts.

5: 2: T15: to read a range of explanatory texts, investigating and noting features of impersonal style, e.g. complex sentences: use of passive voice; technical vocabulary; hypothetical language (*if… then, might when the…*); use of words/phrases to make sequential, causal, logical connections, e.g. *while, during, after, because, due to, only when, so*

The Stars

introductory paragraph presents the subject and preliminary ideas

technical terminology

The stars in the sky look small because they are so far away. In fact they are huge. Each star is a glowing **ball of gases** held together by gravity. Most of this gas **is hydrogen**. In the hot fury of a star's 'core', or centre, hydrogen reaches a temperature of at least 10 million °C.

The birth and death of a star
Stars are born in clusters. A **cloud of gas and dust** called a **nebula** breaks up over millions of years into smaller clouds which are then pulled tighter and smaller by their own gravity. Eventually they heat up and start to shine.

clear and distinct stages

Gravity   Core   Gravity

A star being formed from gas and dust

● After billions of years, stars finally run out of energy and die.

Supernova

Red giant

● The remains of a very large star may collapse to form a black hole.

● Larger stars do not last as long as smaller ones. They die dramatically in an explosion. The exploding star is called a supernova.

● As a star grows old, its core becomes hotter and swells up. This swollen star is called a red giant.

facts brought as close as possible to reader's experience

The heat inside a star changes hydrogen atoms into the atoms of another gas called **helium**.
   When this happens there is an '**atomic reaction**' and a flash of energy is given out. Billions of these flashes of energy keep the star hot and make it shine.
   The **Sun** is the nearest star to Earth. It is only a middle-sized star but it looks big to us because it is so close – only 150 million km away!

Black hole

Pulsar

White dwarf

● A black hole is invisible because light cannot escape from it.

● A very small, extremely dense body is left, called a neutron star.
● Some neutron stars, called pulsars, give off pulses of light and radio waves as they spin.

● Eventually the star collapses and becomes a white dwarf – a small but very hot star. It cools and finally fades away.

temporal connectives denoting the passage of time – sequencing

causal connective denoting cause and effect

5: 2: T16: to prepare for reading by identifying what they already know and what they need to find out

5: 2: T20: notemaking: to discuss what is meant by 'in your own words' and when it is appropriate to copy, quote and adapt

5: 2: W9: to search for, collect, define and spell technical words derived from work in other subjects

The game

P
144

Background

Rather than giving a scientific explanation for a natural process, as in the previous extract, this text explains how a game is played. However, it is different from an instructional text (see 'Pick a Book' trick, page 44), where the reader is told what to do. Here we have explanations of cause and effect – how a foul can cause a free kick, how a kick over the goal line results in a corner, and so on.

Shared reading and discussing the text

● Before reading the text, ask the children to explain the terms *free kick, corner kick* and *penalty*. Can they explain what these are and what causes them? Having done this, ask if anyone can explain the offside rule to the rest of the class. As explanations are offered, keep picking out the points where one thing causes, or is caused by, another. These form the basis of explanation writing.

● Read the text and check the explanations given to you by the children against the ones provided in the text. Ask them to think in terms of what causes what. Can they see examples of one thing causing another (for example, a penalty caused by a foul)? As a piece of shared annotation, look through the text and find examples of causality, circling one thing and then the other in the chain of cause and effect.

● Pick out the language features of an explanation text. Point out the use of terms such as *you* and *your team*. Explain that they don't refer to one specific 'you', they are aimed at anyone reading the text – the language is impersonal. Pick out examples of this use of the second person. Note also the use of connecting language. Ask the children to pick out examples of language showing one thing causing or being caused by another (for example, *if... then* sentences) as well as connectives showing the passage of time (*when, then*).

● Read through the text and ask the children to locate ten sentences that have more than one verb. Gather examples, circling the verbs. In each sentence check whether each verb is in its own clause – a small unit of sense within a sentence. For example, *You are awarded a free kick if you are fouled by the opposition* contains two verbs (*awarded* and *fouled*), each in a clause. Look at the words or punctuation marks that connect the various clauses (in the example above the causal connective *if* performs this task).

Activities

● Ask the children to make a set of cards consisting of 'football' pairs – each pair should have a cause (for example, foul in the area) and an effect (for example, penalty kick). When they have made the cards, they should shuffle them, display them face up, and see if they can reunite causes and effects.

● Using the text, can the children produce a series of diagrams explaining the processes presented? Can they draw a diagram for a free kick, showing, step by step, how it happens? Ask them to try mapping out the offside rule. They could turn their material into a poster about the rules of football.

● Ask the children to read the section on the offside rule and use play figures to try to explain to each other how it works. Ask them to clarify the rule, working in groups of three. Recruit the services of staff who don't understand the rule and see if your pundits can explain it.

Extension/further reading

Ask the children to think of other activities undertaken in PE and explain them. It could be games that they play or routines that they follow when using apparatus.

Children could read books that explain the rules and processes involved in games such as basketball and tennis.

5: 2: T15: to read a range of explanatory texts, investigating and noting features of impersonal style, e.g. complex sentences: use of passive voice; technical vocabulary; hypothetical language (*if… then, might when the…*); use of words/phrases to make sequential, causal, logical connections, e.g. *while, during, after, because, due to, only when, so*

5: 2: W9: to search for, collect, define and spell technical words derived from work in other subjects

5: 2: T16: to prepare for reading by identifying what they already know and what they need to find out

The game

definitions (in brackets) given for technical terms

impersonal language – 'you' and 'your' could refer to anyone

cause and effect ('If…')

complex sentences: clauses joined by connective comma

Free kicks
You are awarded a free kick if you are fouled by the opposition. A free kick can be direct (from which you can score), or indirect (from which you cannot directly score). Direct free kicks are awarded for the more serious offences.

Corner kick
Your team is given a corner kick if the opposition kicks the ball over their own goal line.

Penalty kick
A penalty kick is awarded to the opposition if you commit a foul inside your own penalty area,

irrespective of the position of the ball, provided it is in play. It is a shot at the goal taken from the penalty spot with only the goalkeeper to beat.

Fouls
If a player commits a foul, a free kick is awarded to the opposite team. For persistent rule-breaking, a player is cautioned and shown a yellow card. If a player is shown a yellow card twice they are sent off the field. For serious fouls a player is shown a red card and sent off immediately. In both cases the player cannot be replaced by another player.

Offside rule

The offside rule is devised to stop players loitering around the opposition's goal. You are offside if you are nearer to your opponents' goal line than the ball, when the ball touches or is played by one of your team. It is not an offence to be in an offside position unless you are interfering with play or gaining an advantage, in which case the opposite team gets a free kick. You are not offside if you receive the ball from a throw-in, goal kick, corner kick, or drop ball. You are also not offside if there are two or more opponents between you and the goal line.

connecting language:

causal (causing something)

temporal (related to time)

oppositional (in contrast)

5: 2: S5: to use punctuation effectively to signpost meaning in longer and more complex sentences

5: 2: S9: to secure the use of the comma in embedding clauses within sentences

Danger by Moonlight by Jamila Gavin

Background

Jamila Gavin's adventure story tells of Filippo, who has never seen his father. His father was a jeweller in Venice (he was the creator of a jewelled pendant, 'The Ocean of the Moon') and had journeyed to Hindustan to work for Emperor Shah Jehan. When Filippo was 12, the family learned that his father had been kidnapped. Filippo and his brother Carlo journeyed to India to rescue their father. Years later, when this passage is set, the two brothers return to the palace that has been designed in the likeness of 'The Ocean of the Moon', the Taj Mahal.

There is an old tradition that a jeweller, Geronimo Veronese, designed this great palace. This beautiful passage shows the brothers' feelings as they enter the magnificent building.

Shared reading and discussing the text

● Read through the passage and ask the children where and when they think it is set. Ask them to put forward suggestions and give reasons for these from the text. They can give broad hints as to the type of place where the story is set – they may notice clues such as the call to prayer, the green parrots in the sky, the dome and the atmosphere created by it.

● Give the children some background to the text, noting that the two brothers are entering the palace that is based on a jewel created by their father. Explore some of the specific and cultural features of this setting. Explain to the children that the Adhan is a call to prayer within Islam. It dates back to the time of the Prophet Muhammad and is still called five times a day at prayers. Look also at the way the setting is described over the course of the passage, from the dawn and the first glimpse of what is within the high walls to the brightness of the sun as it climbs in the sky. Ask each child to locate a sentence or phrase that most makes them feel like they are there, with the characters, experiencing these events. Can they relate to the excitement a person can feel when they shut their eyes and open them to make sure things are real?

● Explore the use of time to communicate the brothers' feelings. A few steps are communicated slowly, sentence by sentence, as they pass through the gates and see the dome for the first time. In the last paragraph three hours are accounted for in one sentence. This gives the reader a sense of the stillness, the lack of movement, as the brothers stand in awe for three whole hours.

Activities

● Give the children some starter lines, such as *In this story...The characters see...The characters feel..When I read it I thought...* , so that they can use them to structure a discursive piece of writing about the text.

● Everything happens very gradually in the text, as events unfold, and this helps to heighten the effect the text has on the reader – the *long, long, reverberations* that the brothers hear as they stand outside the gateway; the gatekeepers coming out from under their blankets; the light filtering through onto the scene, and so on. Point out that rather than saying something like *We went through the gate and saw the big dome*, the writer has used her language carefully to build up the atmosphere. Can the children write some other sentences that could slot into this text, adding to the growing sense of awe as the brothers enter the gates? Remind them to use prepositions to make their text read more smoothly, moving forward the events in the story.

● Ask the children to find words in the text that they would like to check in a dictionary. Make a list of these on the board, then ask the children to look them up in a dictionary. They will find this builds up further their stock of dramatic and interesting words they can use in their own writing.

Extension/further reading

The passage can stimulate research work on the Taj Mahal, with potential for a web search to find pictures of the palace today.

Children could research the way prayer is undertaken by Muslims.

5: 3: T1: to investigate a range of texts from different cultures, considering patterns of relationships, social customs, attitudes and beliefs:
● identify these features by reference to the text
● consider and evaluate these features in relation to their own experience

chapter opening gives 'where' and 'when' and description

DANGER BY MOONLIGHT

the setting emerges

exotic noises

calls the believers to prayer (Allah is the greatest, I bear witness there is no god but Allah; Muhammad is Allah's messenger)

flashback reminding the reader of the jewel that would become the design for the Taj Mahal

dark dawn

atmospheric light

shows the feelings of the brothers – the effect that the scene they are observing is having on them

reveals his response

sense of things being unreal

paragraph used for events which are close together, but 1 sentence used for the passing of 3 hours

the use of time when describing the narrator's experience heightens the effect on the reader and helps to portray the characters' feelings

the whiteness, the heat, the stillness, the camels far ahead – all convey the atmosphere

prepositions

location given to fix the setting

So now we stand outside the great arched gateway. It is dawn. Within the high walls, we can see the tops of the trees and clouds of green parrots swooping and screeching as they greet the new day. We hear the call to prayer. The echo reaches us; long, long, reverberations of:

Allahu-Akbar
Ash-hadu-alla-ilaha-illallah
Ash-hadu anna Muhammadar-Rasulullah
Hayya-alassalah
Hayya-alal-Falah
Allahu Akbar
La ilahu illallah

There is a sense of immense peace and goodness. The gatekeepers unroll themselves from their blankets and greet us as we enter the dark green gardens. Night still hangs in shadows and stretches long-fingered across the lawns. The great sky turns silver. Our hearts stop. The light strikes an opaque shape. It is a dome; a vast dome – bigger than any I have ever seen. More and more light pours through a crack in the dawn sky. The dome floats moon-white, like a giant lotus, and lights up the four white

minarets standing like handmaidens at each corner.

Carlo hides his eyes as if he has seen a vision. "Is it really there?" he asks, awestruck.

He looks again. "Yes, yes! It is still there."

But I am silent. I remember Shah Jehan holding The Ocean of the Moon in his fingers, suspended in the candlelight so that the gems were filled with air, fire, water and ice. I seem to see it again now – but huge and overwhelming, as if we stand within the jewel itself. I too shut my eyes, expecting that such beauty cannot be real, that it will have vanished when we open them again. But it hasn't. We stare in utter silence, watching the dawn sliding pale pink over the white marble.

We have been standing for three hours. The sun is riding high in an azure sky, the dome is too white, too bright to look at, but still we stand, dazzled, speaking occasionally in hushed voices. Beyond, we see the glittering River Jamuna, and the fields stretching away to a shimmering horizon. A distant camel train picks its way through the shallows. Life goes on.

5: 3: T2: to identify the point of view from which a story is told and how this affects the reader's response

5: 3: T10: to write discursively about a novel or story, e.g. to describe, explain, or comment on it

5: 3: W12: to use dictionaries efficiently to explore spellings, meanings, derivations, e.g. by using alphabetical order, abbreviations, definitions with understanding

Black Angels

by Rita Murphy

Background

Rita Murphy's novel is set in Georgia in the early 1960s. It concerns Celli – a child who believes she is white, though discovers she has a black grandmother during the course of the story. She is cared for to a large extent by Sophie, the household maid.

Sophie is involved in the civil rights movement and the story is set at a time when the Freedom Riders are travelling through their town. When certain states refused to follow legislation for racial equality, the Freedom Riders travelled on buses, challenging racist regulations that segregated public facilities such as transport and cafés. They were often met with hostility. In this extract Celli meets Sophie from prison, following a riot in the town during the Freedom Riders' visit. This passage is the culmination of a hard night.

Shared reading and discussing the text

● Explain the background to the story and ask the children how they think they would feel if their much loved carer was wrongly taken into prison. How would they expect Celli to react when she meets Sophie from jail? After reading the passage, review the predictions the children have made. How accurate were these?

● A number of features in the passage stem from the culture and events of the times depicted. There are pieces of dialect speech ('*I been gone*'), references to historical events ('*the Klan*') and social customs (Celli tells Sophie she should *know your place*), and the expression of feelings prompted by the situation in which the characters find themselves ('*My people have a chance to take back their power, their dignity,*' says Sophie). Discuss these with the children.

● Read through the text and ask the children to look carefully at the dialogue. Which lines tell the reader something important? What sort of emotions are being expressed by the speakers? Choose a particular section to focus on and ask the children to note who is speaking, how they are talking and what is being said.

● Look at the conflicting points of view expressed in the text. Why do the children think Celli was angry? Ask them to look at what she says and make a list of things that have angered her (and still anger her). They will need to try to explain why Celli has no friends (in the story she fell out with friends who mistreated their maids). Then look at the point of view expressed by Sophie. What does she mean by '*This is bigger than you. It's bigger than any of us*' in her speech beginning '*You think this.*'. ?

Activities

● In this text the relationship between the two characters is fluid – it moves from a stand-off, to anger and confrontation, to concern, to a hug. This is all carried along by the dialogue. Ask the children to imagine the different emotions that could work their way through a conversation between two characters, as the conversation develops. Perhaps a parent is angry with their child for getting lost but then, on finding their child, gradually calms down and explains he was only worried; or maybe someone is overjoyed to see a friend but then realises how jealous she is of their new bike. Ask the children to try structuring their own text in which the conversation carries characters through a string of varied emotions.

● Children can read this passage from Sophie's point of view. How did she feel to be out of jail? What was she thinking as Celli raged? Ask the children to devise some sentences (they don't need to rewrite the passage) that explain how the situation looked and felt from Sophie's point of view.

Extension/further reading

Children can research books on the civil rights movement of the 1960s and the work of Martin Luther King. They could focus on issues raised in this passage, researching the work of the Freedom Riders and the way the civil rights movement led to imprisonment for many of its supporters, including Dr King.

5: 3: T1: to investigate a range of texts from different cultures, considering patterns of relationships, social customs, attitudes and beliefs:
● identify these features by reference to the text
● consider and evaluate these features in relation to their own experience

5: 3: T2: to identify the point of view from which a story is told and how this affects the reader's response

5: 3: T3: to change point of view, e.g. tell incident or describe a situation from the point of view of another character or perspective

features of text from a different culture:

1. dialect used for Sophie's speech

2. reference to historical and cultural features – the civil rights movement, the Klu Klux Klan

3. reveals customs of the people involved in the story – Sophie is expected to know her place

4. expresses the feelings of the character about the culture she is caught up in

Black Angels

"You've had a long day, now, haven't you, Celli?"

I thought that after everything that had happened I would have been glad just to see Sophie alive, but I found myself burning up with anger toward her. "What do you think, Sophie?" I asked, all filled with spit.

"I think you did, missy, and don't use that tone with me. Just 'cause I been gone for one day don't give you the right to talk bad to me."

"You don't know what I've been through tonight, Sophie. You have no idea where I've been." Then the words ran right out of me like a river. "If you weren't involved with this stupid Movement, I wouldn't be here right now getting you out of jail. I wouldn't have been at the Screaming River Church tonight with the Klan throwing fire bottles through the windows. And I'd have a few friends left whose mothers wouldn't be afraid to invite me into their houses. If you could just keep quiet for once, Sophie, and know your place, maybe I could have a normal life".

Sophie sat up taller in her seat. "You think this is all about *you?* Is that what you think? You think because you were inconvenienced tonight, I should stop speaking the truth. You got to wake up, girl! This isn't about you. This is bigger than you. It's bigger than any of us. Can't you see that? My people have a chance to take back their power, their dignity. Nothing is more important to me than that, Celli. Nothing. Do you understand?" I nodded my head. Tears welled up in my eyes and Sophie's, too.

"I'm just tired of worrying about you, Sophie. I worry about you every day. All the time. I thought they killed you today. I thought you were never coming home. Not ever." Sophie wiped a tear from my cheek.

"We all get tired, honey," she said, folding me into her arms. "But we can't give up. Not now."

point of view expressed by character's inner thoughts and feelings

Celli's point of view contrasted with Sophie's

narrative telling us what characters see and feel

points of view coming together at the conclusion

5: 3: T8: to record predictions, questions, reflections while reading, e.g. through the use of a reading journal

5: 3: T9: to write in the style of the author, e.g. writing on to complete a section, resolve a conflict; writing additional dialogue, new chapter

Travellers' Tales

by Anthony Masters

P

147

Background

However tolerant post-war British culture might have become, the traveller community still faces a high degree of prejudice. They lack sites at which they can stay and are harassed as they move from town to town. This harassment is often based on perceptions that travellers are all thieving poachers. Anthony Masters' book, *Travellers' Tales*, charts the adventures of the Roberts family, who are Romanies, and challenges a number of stereotypical images that burden the traveller community as a whole. In this passage, the bailiffs and police evicting the Roberts family from their current site are interrupted as they hear the howl of a police dog caught in a trap. The scene is full of tension.

Shared reading and discussing the text

● Explain the scenario to the children: the travellers are being evicted by the police and bailiffs, and one of the police dogs has got caught in a steel trap. What do they expect the police will be thinking about the trap and the travellers? What assumptions might they make? How might the travellers react? Read the text as far as *The policeman was cynical* and ask the children what they think could happen next. Encourage them to come up with an array of possibilities for the next events in the story, from a bust-up to peace. Keep a copy of these on a large sheet of paper.

● Pick out the way in which the passage has presented experiences from a particular culture. Traveller tensions with the police are communicated in the relationships between the characters. There is also insight into the familiarity travellers can have with their own animals, demonstrated in the natural way in which they soothe the anxious dog.

● Finish reading the extract and ask the children what they think Prim and Billy might be able to do. How will the policemen react to their actions?

Explore the tension around the policemen's assumption that the travellers have set the traps. How would this make the travellers feel?

● What clues are given regarding the thoughts and feelings of the various characters in the text? Reading through the passage twice, once for the police and once for the travellers, annotate the text, underlining words or phrases that indicate the point of view different characters are adopting, and note down the reactions they are encountering. Note the sarcasm of the police and the restraining of tempers by the travellers.

● Ask the children to look for various uses of the apostrophe in the text, including some uses for contraction (*don't, it's*) and some for possession (*dog's, poachers'*). The example *poachers'* provides a good opportunity to explore how apostrophes are used with plural nouns.

Activities

● Ask the children to work in writing groups of three, examining the roles of characters from the story – one could look at the cynical policeman, another Reuben, and a third Prim. Ask them to imagine the scene right at the end of the extract. To do this they will need to read the text, noting what their character has said and how he or she has reacted to the words of others. Having done this, they should write down the thoughts that they think are running through their character's head at the end of the passage.

● Remaining in their threes, the children can take it in turns to go into their selected role and be interviewed by the other two children in their group, who pose questions that have to be answered in role (for example, *'What did you think of the way the policeman spoke to you?'*).

● Ask the children to work through the passage to find as many different punctuation marks as they can, examining why they are being used. They should annotate a copy of the text by circling these.

5: 3: T1: to investigate a range of texts from different cultures, considering patterns of relationships, social customs, attitudes and beliefs:
● identify these features by reference to the text
● consider and evaluate these features in relation to their own experience

5: 3: T2: to identify the point of view from which a story is told and how this affects the reader's response

5: 3: T3: to change point of view, e.g. tell incident or describe a situation from the point of view of another character or perspective

TRAVELLERS' TALES

Extract 1

The scene in the woods was tragic. The big Alsatian was lying on the ground, its paw in a cruel steel trap. Two policemen were kneeling beside the animal and one of them was stroking its head while it howled plaintively. Of Horace and the other policeman there was no sign. Reuben, Prim, Billy and Len knelt down beside the dog.

"It's one of the big-uns," said Reuben.

"This your work?" demanded the policeman brusquely.

"Poachers," muttered Reuben.

"Oh yeah?" The policeman was cynical.

"Take it or leave it – this is poachers' work. But I don't expect you to believe me. And don't do *that*!"

The dog gave an anguished howl and the policeman dropped its paw, which he'd been trying to squeeze out of the trap.

"What the—? *You* got any ideas?"

"Yes we have," said Billy. "Shall I go and get the grease, Dad?"

"OK."

He ran off.

"We've done this before," said Prim.

"I bet you have," said the other policeman bitterly. "Getting a nice fat rabbit out, were we? Or a pheasant?"

"We never—"

But Reuben interrupted her. "Ignore him, love. He doesn't know our ways. What's the dog's name?"

"Sam," said the other policeman grudgingly.

"OK, Prim – do your stuff," said Reuben quietly.

shows policeman's attitude

traveller's response

text shows different points of view

the travellers and the policemen are facing the same situation but dealing with it differently

cultural features: travellers in conflict with the police and bailiffs

traveller's action

apostrophe used for contraction

apostrophe used for possession

policeman hesitant about giving the dog's name

5: 3: S4: to use punctuation marks accurately in complex sentences

5: 3: S5: to revise use of apostrophes for possession (from Y4 term 1)

Travellers' Tales

by Anthony Masters

Extract 2

Background

Continuing Anthony Masters' *Travellers' Tales*, in this extract the skill with which Prim handles the dog and the sensitivity with which the traveller family handle the poacher trap brings a change to the attitudes adopted by the policemen and bailiffs at the scene.

Stories that explore a range of cultures can challenge stereotypes and present insights into diverse ways and lives. This example builds on Reuben's words in the earlier extract. In response to a derogatory remark by one of the policemen that wound up Prim, he remarked: *'Ignore him, love. He doesn't know our ways.'*

Anthony Masters gained his understanding of the ways of this culture from his years spent working with traveller children.

Shared reading and discussing the text

● Before reading the text, recall where the story left off in the previous extract and revise the work done on how the different characters were reacting to one another. Review the list of predictions that the children made halfway through the reading of the first extract. How do they think the situation might turn out now?

● Read the whole passage and ask the children to look for the turning points in the story. At what points does the tension change? Are there particular sections where characters respond differently from how they responded before? Ask the children to re-read the extract and each select three turning points in the text (invite a few children to annotate the displayed class version of the text, putting a small slash through each of their selected sections). What reasons can the children give for choosing those particular lines of text?

● Draw four parallel lines on the board labelled *Reuben, Prim, dog-handler* and *other policeman*. Encourage the children to contribute to some notes you make about each character that indicate what the characters are doing, thinking and feeling, as the story progresses. For example, the notes for Prim could include the phrase *strokes dog*; the dog-handler's could include the phrase *suddenly shows respect for Prim*).

● Briefly revisit the use of the apostrophe to denote the possessive of a singular word (*Alsatian's*) in this extract, contrasting it with its use in plural words in the previous extract (*poachers'*).

Activities

● Ask the children to retell the story, adopting the point of view of either the cynical policeman or the dog-handler. How would each character describe the way in which Prim handles the dog and Billy eases its paw? What about the patient response of Reuben, in spite of all the goading that takes place? Before writing, ask each child to plan out a retelling from each of these points of view and then select the one they want to write up.

● Drawing on their own experience, can the children think of a time when they were in trouble but hadn't actually done anything? Ask them to recount the event, particularly highlighting what was said and how the speech of the participants indicated what they were thinking or feeling about the situation.

● Suggest that the children write Prim or Billy's diary for that day. How would they recount the events that took place and what descriptions would they give of each of the policemen?

Extension/further reading

A number of LEAs have traveller support services who can provide information and speakers to give further insight into traveller life in the UK. Other novels by Anthony Masters include those in the *Police Dog* series (Bloomsbury).

5: 3: T1: to investigate a range of texts from different cultures, considering patterns of relationships, social customs, attitudes and beliefs:
● identify these features by reference to the text
● consider and evaluate these features in relation to their own experience

5: 3: T2: to identify the point of view from which a story is told and how this affects the reader's response

5: 3: T3: to change point of view, e.g. tell incident or describe a situation from the point of view of another character or perspective

TRAVELLERS' TALES
Extract 2

She began to stroke the dog, whispering his name over and over again. "Sam – dear old Sam. Sam. You'll be all right, my dear." The dog turned and fastened its eyes on her. "You'll be all right – my dear Sam."

A few moments later Billy came leaping back with the grease. "All right, Billy boy – go ahead."

Billy began to spread it on the Alsatian's paw, and as he did so Prim kept stroking the dog and saying, "Come on, my dearie. It's going to be all right. My dear Sam – you're going to be all right."

The dog-handler looked at her with a new respect in his eyes. "You've got on the right side of him and all."

But the other policeman remained unconvinced. "Don't let them get round you, Derek. You know they're only springing their own traps."

Len continued to spread the grease gently.

Then Reuben said, "Prim, take his paw." She did as she was told, still talking gently and now caressing Sam with her other hand. "Now pull!"

With a very swift movement she pulled. Sam gave a little whimper and his paw was out. He lay down, panting, and licking at the paw.

"Best carry him back," said Reuben. "I reckon that's broken."

"Well I'll be damned." They looked up to see that quite a crowd of bailiffs and Travellers had gathered. And one of the bailiffs was gazing at the Roberts in reluctant admiration. "I've never seen the like of that."

travellers' excellent ability in handling dogs and dealing with injury

apostrophe used for possession

turning point

text shows varied points of view and what the characters (travellers, policemen and bailiffs) are doing, thinking and feeling

reveals change in attitude

5: 3: S4: to use punctuation marks accurately in complex sentences

Anancy

by James Berry

Background

Anancy is the Spiderman of African Caribbean folk tradition. He is a trickster in a story world inhabited by animal characters such as Bro Dog and Bro Monkey. In this extract he encounters his enemy, Bro Tiger. The character of Anancy originated in Ghana, West Africa, as tales of an Ashanti spider god. It is never clear in this tradition how like a spider or how like a man he actually is – the two are intertwined. What is clear is the trickery. He is constantly outwitting the other characters in his encounters with them.

Shared reading and discussing the text

● Introduce the characters in the extract and talk about the idea of the magic stools – anyone who counts all ten in one go will die. This mythical notion can be compared with the warning Orpheus was given: turn round and Eurydice returns to the world of the dead (see page 50). Tell the children that immediately before this episode Anancy has heard Tiger try this out on Rabbit, with Rabbit suffering the fatal consequences. Ask them what they think Anancy could do to try to outwit Tiger. They may reason that he needs to get Tiger to count to ten – the question is, how to do this?

● Read the extract up to when Anancy counts the stools for the first time (lines 19/20). Ask the children if they have any inkling what Anancy is up to. Why does he laugh? How might Tiger react to this? Recall the Till Owlyglass extract (see page 54) and the tug of war in 'Hare, Hippo and Elephant' (see page 52) in which readers gradually gain some idea of what the trickster is up to. Read through the extract to the end. Can the children identify how Anancy has managed to trick Tiger? How has the trick worked? Why has Tiger counted the magic stools?

● Review some of the cultural features of this extract. There is the use of dialect terms such as

Bro and *vex*. There is also the inclusion of a common element in folklore from various cultures – the magic spell. It is told in the present tense, which give the effects of a storyteller taking us through the scene as it unfolds.

● Look at the paragraph that begins *Anancy laughs at how clever…* In these sentences we are given an insight into Anancy's thoughts; the story is narrated in a way that shows it from his point of view. Ask the children to imagine similar sentences that could be slotted in to show what Anancy is thinking elsewhere in the story. Can they inject a similar sense of what a main character is thinking about events into their writing?

Activities

● Ask the children to take ten sentences (they will all be in the present tense) and reword them, either orally or in writing, as past tense sentences. Can they spell the newly formed past tense verbs they are using?

● Terms such as *fool-fool man* and *getting vex* are examples of terminology that root the tale in a particular tradition. Ask the children to list words and expressions that they think could be less familiar to some readers.

● Can the children create a short drama which shows Anancy's trick? They will need to consider the actions, tones of voice and facial expressions of both Anancy and Tiger as they act it out. Ask them to use their scripting skills (developed in term 1) to write out the conversation.

Extension/further reading

Ask the children to compare this story with the one about Till Owlyglass (see page 54). Can they think of other stories in which a trick is played?

The other retellings of Anancy tales, from James Berry (Walker Books), all contain a fun element and are similarly rich in language.

5: 3: T1: to investigate a range of texts from different cultures, considering patterns of relationships, social customs, attitudes and beliefs:
● identify these features by reference to the text
● consider and evaluate these features in relation to their own experience

5: 3: T6: to explore the challenge and appeal of older literature through:
● listening to older literature being read aloud
● reading accessible poems, stories and extracts
● reading extracts from classic serials shown on television
● discussing differences in language used

Anancy

present tense used for telling the story, as used in joke telling

Getting up to meet Tiger, Anancy greets him sweet-sweet. "Good afternoon, Bro Tiger."

"What d'you want?" Tiger says. "I'm in charge here."

"Mister King Tiger, I see you are in charge."

"I'm glad you see that. I'm glad you see you should call me Mister King Tiger."

"Position can make a man a big-big man."

shows us what sort of relationship Tiger expects – people should respect him like a king

"I'm doing a prize, with the gold stool. You're good at good-luck, and a bit of brain. Come. Try it."

"You know I'm not an educated man," Anancy says.

"I get on. You see that. Copy me. Hear what I say. Win the gold stool."

Anancy laughs at how clever Bro Tiger thinks he has become. He knows Tiger believes he'll count the stools and die. But Anancy doesn't say he knows Tiger thinks that. Instead, Anancy says, "You mean if I win I'll have gold and be rich. And you will be a king already. So both of us can be proud and be good friends. Do you mean that?"

spell in the story: counting the stools (1 to 10) leads to death

gives insight into the character of Anancy

"Yes. Yes." Tiger answers without thinking. Impatient, he goes on. "Come on then. Come. Count the stools. All of them in one go."

Anancy counts, "One. Two. Three. Four. Five. Six. Seven. Eight. Nine. And one more."

Tiger looks up surprised, puzzled and then gets cross. "That isn't proper counting."

"All right, Mister King Tiger. It's not a time to burn yourself out getting vex, I can try again."

dialect for 'annoyed'

"Right. But better this time. Better this time."

Anancy counts again. "One. Two. Three. Four. Five. Six. Seven. Eight. And two more."

explains what Anancy is doing and how the trick works

Tiger leaps up and stamps about in a rage. "Stupid, fool-fool man. Stupid, fool-fool man. Can't count! Can't count properly!" Tiger turns round in his rage, carried away with his anger. He points to the stools, saying, "Fool-fool man, count like this, One. Two. Three. Four. Five. Six. Seven. Eight. Nine. Ten." Tiger drops down, rolls over, dead, showing his belly.

reader finds out why Anancy was laughing earlier

The Three Magi

by Stanislaw Baranczak

Background

The poetry of Eastern Europe during Communist rule contains many examples of poems of protest. This example depicts the experience of a visit by the state police. The imagery used is the visit of the three kings in the New Testament (which also underpins 'Journey of the Magi', see page 66).

Stanislaw Baranczak was born in Poland in 1946, and his works span from the Communist era to the present day. His writing often reflects his political and human rights concerns.

Shared reading and discussing the text

● Read through the poem twice. On the second reading, ask the children to focus on the three visitors and what they actually do. Encourage the children to read the poem slowly, examining sentences and the detail around them (for example, *The star of an ID will flash before your eyes*). Encourage the children to use the commas as a pointer, signalling an added piece of description or action, for example. Reading the text in this way will help them to gather a more accurate impression of what is taking place in the poem. After they have done this, ask the children who they think the visitors in the poem are and what they think happens to the person receiving the visit.

● Read the sentence *Since that time…* and look at how each verb is set within a separate clause. Each clause adds another change that has taken place in the old friend who now stands at the door of this house. The same structure can be seen in the sentence *The gold of their watches…*

● Explain some of the imagery in the text by reminding the children of the visit of the three Magi in Matthew 2: 1–12. They brought gold (a precious metal used in jewellery and commerce for thousands of years and valued for its beauty and resilience), frankincense (a white-coloured resin, one of the most costly substances in the ancient world, used in medicines and incense) and myrrh (a dark resin used in perfumes, incense and embalming, taken as a symbol of sad and

bitter experience). Next, explain the situation in former Soviet bloc countries – something which is still the case in oppressive regimes – in which a secret police can operate above the law and curtail people's freedom. Finally, explain that forceps are sometimes still used by midwives and doctors to help guide a baby's head down the birth canal.

● Reflect on what this experience would be like in real life. Ask the children to visualise the early morning call, the visitor barging in and taking away a member of the family. Can they think of other things that might happen – words that could be said, people who could be woken up, perhaps things that might be broken – in such circumstances? And what about the significance of the last line, *Wasn't this a vast world*? Do the children have any ideas about what it means? Is the world that he once knew now in the past?

Activities

● Ask the children to revisit the three symbols of gold, frankincense and myrrh and write a brief note on how each of these features in the poem. How does the myrrh, in particular, connect with these events?

● Encourage the children to create their own poem about a situation like this. They will be fortunate not to be living in a police state, but can they imagine what it would be like and how such an event would unfold?

● Ask the children to annotate a copy of the poem, highlighting parts about which they have something to say. These could be reflections on the images used or ideas of their own about this experience. Then ask them to write an introductory paragraph that presents the poem to a new reader. What would they say about it?

Extension/further reading

Children could research into the work of groups like Amnesty International, who campaign over issues of justice for political prisoners. Amnesty provide resources to prompt letter writing to various governments on such issues.

5: 3: T1: to investigate a range of texts from different cultures, considering patterns of relationships, social customs, attitudes and beliefs:
● identify these features by reference to the text
● consider and evaluate these features in relation to their own experience

5: 3: T10: to write discursively about a novel or story, e.g. to describe, explain, or comment on it

5: 3: T5: to select poetry, justify their choices, e.g. in compiling class anthology

THE THREE MAGI

To Lech Dymarski

They will probably come just after the New Year.
As usual, early in the morning.
The forceps of the door bell will pull you out by the head
from under the bedclothes; dazed as a newborn baby,
you'll open the door. The star of an ID
will flash before your eyes.
Three men. In one of them you'll recognise
with sheepish amazement (isn't this a small
world) your schoolmate of years ago.
Since that time he'll hardly have changed,
only grown a moustache,
perhaps gained a little weight.
They'll enter. The gold of their watches will glitter (isn't
this a grey dawn), the smoke from their cigarettes
will fill the room with a fragrance like incense.
All that's missing is myrrh, you'll think half-consciously—
while with your heel you're shoving under the couch the book they mustn't find—
what is this myrrh, anyway,
you'd have to finally look it up
someday. You'll come
with us, sir. You'll go
with them. Isn't this a white snow.
Isn't this a black Fiat.
Wasn't this a vast world.

Stanislaw Baranczak

challenging imagery

what must it be like for 2 school friends to be in this situation?

a verb in each clause

the reader's visualisation of the scene grows with each clause

nativity images

sudden change to past tense leaves unanswered questions

5: 3: S6: to investigate clauses through:
● identifying the main clause in a long sentence
● investigating sentences which contain more than one clause
● understanding how clauses are connected (e.g. by combining three short sentences into one)

Morning

by Dionne Brand

Background

Trinidadian poet, Dionne Brand's poem 'Morning' is from the anthology *Can I Buy a Slice of Sky?* It originally featured in her book *Man of Many Colours*. In this poem the day is pictured as someone arriving on a bus. Accompanied by two friends, the day makes her way through a deserted street and then on towards the sea and the sky. With this meeting, the day arrives.

Shared reading and discussing the text

● Read through the text with the children and ask them to explain what has happened in the poem. Establish that night has turned into morning. Focus on the character of Day and make a list together of the different things she does and the effects she has on those she 'meets'. (You could explain that this is a piece of personification.) Discuss specific characters, such as the rooster and the fisherman, and details in the setting (for example, *red streaks in the corners of the dusty sky*) which help to set the scene, the reader visualising events.

● The poem doesn't tell us who the two friends are; prompt the children to suggest who they might be. There are no right answers. Encourage them to think of friends who are not people (they might be the characters of Sadness and Happiness, perhaps, or Month and Year).

● Work through the poem, and in finding the various things that happen in it, locate the prepositions that are used – words like *in, into, from* and *by* give direction to the different actions. Ask the children to find as many prepositions as they can.

● Do the children like the poem? Can they choose three or four lines that would be their favourite quotation from it? They could try to learn a section by heart.

Activities

● Ask the children to annotate their own copy of the poem, identifying the things Day does and how morning gradually takes form, from Day's first entrance *on an old brown bus* to the flood of light at the end, when there can be no turning back (*The sky… might have changed its mind, but day had come*). Can the children pinpoint the different images that are added on like a jigsaw, one by one, as the poem progresses, so that eventually there is a complete picture? How do these images work?

● Ask the children to draw the character of Day, as a person, and label their picture, pointing out different features. They may like to include aspects of the poem that present the reader with a visual picture of Day, such as the way she bends over to sweep away the dawn and the broom she uses, as well as incorporating their own ideas – is she young or old, for example? There may also be their own imaginative uses of the general theme of the poem – morning – such as day carrying the sun under one arm.

● Taking the four sentences starting from *With her broom…*, the children should be able to identify a number of clauses in each sentence, connected by commas. Ask them to read through this section of the poem and, as a group, agree on which word they consider to be the main verb of each sentence. Can they also spot the conjunctions (*and* and *but*) connecting some of the clauses?

Extension/further reading

Grace Nichols' two collections *Can I Buy a Slice of Sky?* (Knight) and *Poetry Jump-up* (Puffin Books) are well worth reading and contain poems that can be examined in similar ways to 'Morning'.

5: 3: T1: to investigate a range of texts from different cultures, considering patterns of relationships, social customs, attitudes and beliefs:
● identify these features by reference to the text
● consider and evaluate these features in relation to their own experience

5: 3: S4: to use punctuation marks accurately in complex sentences

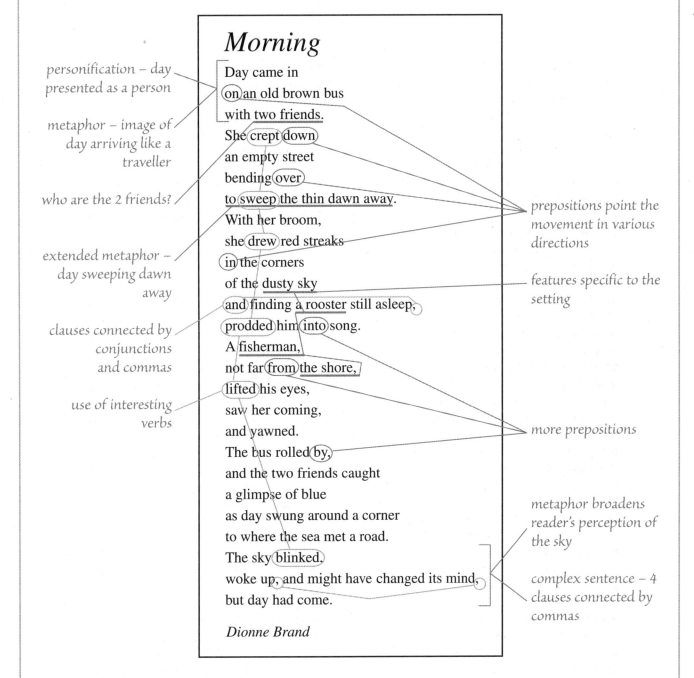

personification – day presented as a person

metaphor – image of day arriving like a traveller

who are the 2 friends?

extended metaphor – day sweeping dawn away

clauses connected by conjunctions and commas

use of interesting verbs

Morning

Day came in
on an old brown bus
with two friends.
She crept down
an empty street
bending over
to sweep the thin dawn away.
With her broom,
she drew red streaks
in the corners
of the dusty sky
and finding a rooster still asleep,
prodded him into song.
A fisherman,
not far from the shore,
lifted his eyes,
saw her coming,
and yawned.
The bus rolled by,
and the two friends caught
a glimpse of blue
as day swung around a corner
to where the sea met a road.
The sky blinked,
woke up, and might have changed its mind,
but day had come.

Dionne Brand

prepositions point the movement in various directions

features specific to the setting

more prepositions

metaphor broadens reader's perception of the sky

complex sentence – 4 clauses connected by commas

5: 3: S6: to investigate clauses through:
● identifying the main clause in a long sentence
● investigating sentences which contain more than one clause
● understanding how clauses are connected (e.g. by combining three short sentences into one)

5: 3: S3: to search for, identify and classify a range of prepositions: *back, up, down, across, through, on,* etc.; experiment with substituting different prepositions and their effect on meaning. Understand and use the term *preposition*

Tao Te Ching

by Lao Tzu

Background

The *Tao Te Ching* is a collection of 81 poems, sayings and words of wisdom. It offers advice on how to understand and lead a good and meaningful life. Written by Lao Tzu in the 5th century BC, the *Tao Te Ching* is central to the religion of Taoism, of which Lao Tzu was a founder. Taoism teaches that life is a journey and that we can find the 'Way' to understanding ourselves and life.

In his poems, Lao Tzu writes about the tensions between living a true or false life. He states that we can learn the skills needed to become better people if we can learn to understand the virtues of justice and truth in all our daily activities. By practising this skill, we gain inner moral strength. This strength allows us to observe ourselves, others and the world with greater tolerance and love. Eventually we are able to find peace and contentment because we have freedom from the mental and emotional suffering caused by overcomplicating our lives with our minds.

This poem (Chapter 54 of the *Tao Te Ching*) explores the idea of growing goodness (*Virtue*). It presents the idea that well-cultivated goodness will last.

Shared reading and discussing the text

● Ask the children to read through the poem, then re-read it to find lines that they can explain or give an opinion about to the rest of the group. As they do this, underline the sections being clarified.

● What do the children understand by the word *Virtue*? Can they also explain the word *cultivate*? Give the definitions that can be applied here (*Virtue* – 'goodness', *cultivate* – 'grow'). Explain that the poem is about developing goodness – can they see the 'growth' of Virtue in the second stanza? Ask them to look at the last word in each line and use dictionaries to define them. Point out the connection between the concept of growth and the word *abundant*.

● Reading the stanza *Therefore look at...*, explain to the children that here we have the idea of taking something at face value as the best way of appreciating and understanding it. The poem is urging us to look at things as they are, accepting them as they appear. Linking back to the third line of the poem, this way of seeing things can then be passed on to the next generation. Developing the theme of looking at *the village as village*, can the children give examples of ways in which their own family or community might seem hard to understand to an outsider?

Activities

● Ask the children to write their own Tao poem based on what they see around them. They must try to keep emotions and overcomplicated thought out of the poem. They could focus on fairness or maintaining a positive attitude in life, as discussed in PSHE and citizenship. Encourage the children to adopt the same style as Lao Tzu in which there are different patterns of repeated words.

● How can virtue be cultivated? How can goodness be spread? In what ways can it be passed on in families and villages? Ask the children to think of four main ways in which virtue can be cultivated in families or nations. They could write down their thoughts on a large sheet of paper to make a poster entitled 'Ways of cultivating virtue'.

● Ask the children to write a short paragraph explaining how the last two lines fit in with the rest of the poem. Discuss their ideas. Establish that the last line reinforces the main idea of the poem – that the key to leading a fulfilled life, one in which you have a powerful insight into its meaning, is to *look* at it in a simple and true way.

Extension/further reading

An ancient text like this provides a fascinating starting point for using web-based search engines. Ask the children to search the Internet for different versions of the *Tao Te Ching* and translations.

5: 3: T1: to investigate a range of texts from different cultures, considering patterns of relationships, social customs, attitudes and beliefs:
● identify these features by reference to the text
● consider and evaluate these features in relation to their own experience

5: 3: T9: to write in the style of the author, e.g. writing on to complete a section, resolve a conflict; writing additional dialogue, new chapter

Tao Te Ching

What is firmly established cannot be uprooted.
What is firmly grasped cannot slip away.
It will be honoured from generation to generation.

Cultivate Virtue in yourself,
And Virtue will be real.
Cultivate it in the family,
And Virtue will abound.
Cultivate it in the village,
And Virtue will grow.
Cultivate it in the nation,
And Virtue will be abundant.
Cultivate it in the universe,
And Virtue will be everywhere.

Therefore look at the body as body;
Look at the family as family;
Look at the village as village;
Look at the nation as nation;
Look at the universe as universe.

How do I know the universe is like this?
By looking!

Lao Tzu

words connected with the theme of growth

let goodness develop/grow

list of good things shows tiers of growth (Virtue grows by starting with the self – once it has been made real by a person it can then spread outwards to other areas)

the village was the most common social unit

keep it simple and look at it just as it is

a village is a village, there is no need to overcomplicate things

the importance of looking, but looking at things in the correct way

5: 3: T6: to explore the challenge and appeal of older literature through:
● listening to older literature being read aloud
● reading accessible poems, stories and extracts
● reading extracts from classic serials shown on television
● discussing differences in language used

Picnic Poem

by David Harmer

Background

David Harmer is a poet and teacher who is part of the Spill The Beans performance team, performing in a range of schools. This poem is a classic example of a poem written for performance, containing language that is excellent for performers to say aloud, repeated refrains that lend themselves to audience participation and a storyline that presents the sort of scenario that will appeal to listeners in its familiarity.

Shared reading and discussing the text

● Ask the children to think of times when a special day out has gone wrong. What went wrong and what happened as a result? Can they remember how the grown-ups involved behaved on these occasions?

● Read through the text and ask the children to pick out all the interesting uses of sound in the poem. Annotate the text as the children provide you with examples. Differentiate between the words which are used to show the noise the car is making (*Crunch bang*) and the words which make up the rest of the poem and are used because of the effect of their sound (for example, the repetition of *car* in blocks of four lines).

● Which parts of the poem do the children think the audience could join in with, as it is spoken aloud? Ask them to read through the poem and select stanzas that they think would be appropriate. Can they think of lively ways in which their chosen lines could be chanted? Encourage them to share their ideas, which can then be tried by the whole group. Begin with the *In our car...* refrains, then move on to the two *Crunch bang...* sections.

● Connect words that rhyme (*day, highway; boot, route* and so on). These can give a sharpness to the performance of a poem and enable the reader to learn the lines more easily. As you make links between each pair of rhyming words, ask the children if they can think of other words with a similar rhyme. They might be able to devise a new line for the poem.

Activities

● Ask the children to use their own experience to write a performance poem in the same vein as 'Picnic Poem'. Suggest that they start with an event – something going wrong or something being a mess – and think of noises associated with the event and how different people felt at the time. Ask them to create a repeated refrain, as in the poem here.

● Work with the class to prepare 'Picnic Poem' for performance (it could be taught to the whole school). Can they make the sounds of the words come alive, while retaining the rhythm of the poem (point out the pattern of the syllables in the first four lines and how a line of many syllables near the end of the poem – *We'll be stuck here...* – suddenly drops down to six again with the next line)? Decide who will say which lines, and encourage the children to think about details such as how they are going to ask the question *What's that?*, each time it occurs. How are they going to convey the change of mood, as the poem progresses?

● The poem is long but memorable. As a class, learn it to enable a better performance – and learn it because it is fun. You could begin with the repeated refrains that the audience can join in with, then the four other stanzas could be spoken by pairs or groups of children who have learned those specific lines.

Extension/further reading

Ask the children to each find four to eight lines of poetry that they don't currently know by heart and learn them.

In addition to David Harmer and Paul Cookson's *Spill The Beans*, Paul Cookson's *Unzip Your Lips* (both published by Macmillan Children's Books) provides a wealth of performance poetry.

5: 3: T4: to read, rehearse and modify performance of poetry

5: 3: T11: to use performance poems as models to write and to produce poetry in polished forms through revising, redrafting and presentation

PICNIC POEM

pattern of syllables used to create a rhythm

[6] In our car in our car
[5] In our c-c-car
[6] In our car in our car
[6] In our wonderful car

We're up and away it's a beautiful day
Zooming along down the main highway
Dad at the wheel picnic in the boot
Sunlight and laughter planning the route.

In our car in our car
In our c-c-car
In our car in our car
In our wonderful car

Crunch bang, What's that?
Crunch bang, What's that?
A whistle and a knock [1] a thumping shock [1]
A whining fizz and a crack on the block [1]
A rattle and splutter [2] a groaning mutter [2]
Cuts through the racket like a knife through butter. [2]

That's our car that's our car
That's our wonderful car
That's our car that's our car
That's our Shhhhhhhhhhhhh

Crunch bang, What's that?
Crunch bang, What's that?
A shove and a kick, dad's got a stick
And he's banging on the engine cos it makes him sick
A mallet and a crowbar, to try to make it go far
He'd be better off trying to drive my Granny's sofa

We've stopped, we're stuck, we're out of luck
Waiting for the man with the breakdown truck
Out with the picnic up with the bonnet
We'll be stuck here for hours you can bet your life upon it

In our car in our car
In our c-c-car
In our car in our car
In our useless car

David Harmer

encourages audience expectation

mood changes through the poem, from happy, to surprised, to angry, to sad

differing lengths of lines and syllables

audience could join in with this repeated refrain

pattern of repeated lines and repeated stanzas

audience could join in by shouting these words

rhyme scheme of rhyming couplets with internal rhymes (for performance)

Stopping by Woods on a Snowy Evening
by Robert Frost

Background

Unlike the previous example, this poem was not written with performance in mind, but it is a poem that works well when spoken aloud to an audience. Robert Frost (1874–1963) wrote a number of poems that drew upon the rural life of New England and reflected the rhythm and vocabulary of American speech. This is one of his most famous poems.

Shared reading and discussing the text

● Read through the poem once. Contrast the first and fourth stanzas with the second and third. Can the children see how the outer stanzas tell us about the traveller, whereas the middle stanzas focus on the horse? In the first and third stanzas, what are the traveller's feelings about the woods? The poet gradually builds up an image of this solitary traveller and his surroundings. Establish that the woods – with their stillness and peace – are a special place for him. Why might he have stopped on his journey? Where do they think he might be going? What are his *promises to keep*?

● In the second and third stanzas, what is the horse's reaction to the traveller stopping at this place? Can the children see that the first and second lines of the second and third stanzas tell us that the horse wonders why they have stopped? Even though the emphasis in these middle stanzas is on the horse, the lines also convey the atmosphere in the woods – the quiet darkness and the lightly falling snow.

● Ask the children to read through the text and tap out the metre of the lines, gently. They will begin to notice the eight syllables. Share ideas on how they think these lines could be said, inviting children to speak specific lines aloud. Help them to spot the shift from a description of the scene (…*The darkest evening of the year*) to the sudden movement of the horse (*He gives his harness bells a shake…*) to the summing up at the end (*The woods are…*), broken by the line starting with the connective *But…* Can they reflect all this in the way they say the lines?

● Reflect on the setting of the poem. Encourage the children to recap on what the woods would look and sound like. Circle the adjectives used in the poem to describe the lake (*frozen*), evening (*darkest*), wind (*easy*), snowflakes (*downy*) and woods (*lovely, dark, deep*).

● Discuss the rhyme scheme the poet uses: in the first stanza the first, second and fourth lines rhyme (*know, though, snow*), and the third line (*here*) then rhymes with the first, second and fourth lines of the next stanza (*queer, near, year*). This pattern is repeated until the final stanza, in which all the lines rhyme. Why do the children think the third line (*And miles to go before I sleep*) is repeated? Point out that the repetition helps to emphasise the long journey ahead of the traveller – this is a quiet moment of reflection for him before he sets off again on the path life takes him.

Activities

● Ask the children to work in groups of eight to prepare the poem for performance. Explain that they should focus on communicating the 'music' of the lines as well as the feelings expressed by the narrator – for example, the tension between going and staying in the final stanza. Help them to structure the poem into different 'moods': the sense of quietness; the scene from the horse's point of view; the feeling of the traveller being resigned to his task ahead at the end.

● When they have worked out the details of their performance, as a group, each child can then annotate their poem, with notes about who is speaking which lines (for example, *Naomi and Imran say this*) and how the lines are going to be spoken (for example, *sounds tired*).

Extension/further reading

In his famous poem, 'The Road Not Taken', Robert Frost tells how *Two roads diverged in a wood, and I – I took the one less travelled by, And that has made all the difference*. The wood in this poem is also a place of quietness and beauty, and where paths (in life) present us with choices. The children could try to work out the meaning of those last three lines of the poem.

5: 3: T4: to read, rehearse and modify performance of poetry

makes the reader wonder why someone would stop

stanza focuses on the traveller

builds up the sense of a solitary traveller

stanzas focus on the horse

builds up the sense of a solitary traveller

adjectives help to create the setting

stanza focuses on the traveller

connective that changes what has gone before

8 beats in each line of poem

rhyme scheme – lines 1, 2 and 4 rhyme

the 3rd line rhymes with lines 1, 2 and 4 of the next stanza

presents an image of the woods – darkness and silence

in 4th stanza all 4 lines rhyme

repetition of line

STOPPING BY WOODS ON A SNOWY EVENING

Whose woods these are I think I know.[1]
His house is in the village though;[2]
He will not see me stopping here[3]
To watch his woods fill up with snow.[4]

My little horse must think it queer[1]
To stop without a farmhouse near[2]
Between the woods and frozen lake[3]
The darkest evening of the year.[4]

He gives his harness bells a shake[1]
To ask if there is some mistake.[2]
The only other sound's the sweep
Of easy wind and downy flake.[4]

The woods are lovely, dark and deep,[1]
But I have promises to keep,[2]
And miles to go before I sleep,[3]
And miles to go before I sleep.[4]

Robert Frost

5: 3: T6: to explore the challenge and appeal of older literature through:
● listening to older literature being read aloud
● reading accessible poems, stories and extracts
● reading extracts from classic serials shown on television
● discussing differences in language used

Sport on TV

Background

The *Radio Times* makes a regular feature of its thought-provoking letters page, carefully structuring letters around specific themes raised by individual programmes. The issue of the amount of sport on television is regularly debated and, in Summer 2002, the combination of the World Cup, Masters Golf and Commonwealth Games and Wimbledon was too much for some viewers. Jeffrey Butcher's letter is one example of this. This text contains some of the main features of a persuasive text: the use of words and phrases to hammer home a point of view, the use of rhetorical questions and an awareness of situations in which other points of view may need to prevail.

Shared reading and discussing the text

● Ask the children to read the text and, in one sentence, sum up the opinion of the writer. Explain that a good persuasive text should leave us in no doubt as to its intention. Having found the writer's main point, ask the class to decide whether they are for or against the viewpoint expressed in the letter. Pick out the arguments Jeffrey makes against the amount of sport on TV.

● Identify the features of a persuasive text in this letter. There is a clearly stated opinion supported by separate points. Note the use of powerful words or phrases (*obsession, destroyed...*) to catch the attention of the reader and put forward the case presented. There is also the anticipation of the objections of others, when points against the writer's case might be stated (*except when made necessary by...*). The letter ends with a rhetorical question – this tries to persuade the reader to agree with the writer's point of view (that the volume of sport on TV should be reduced).

● Compare this text with Term 1's DVLA leaflet (see page 40). Both want to make something happen. What differences can the children see between the two? Ask them to consider the tone of the texts, the relationship between reader and writer and the extent to which the views being presented have to be justified.

Activities

● In two shared sessions, make some notes outlining two different letters. One should argue that there is too much sport on TV, the other should argue that there is the right amount (or alternatively, not enough). Ask the children to give reasons for the viewpoint being adopted and to anticipate and counter arguments against it. They may want to canvass opinions of school adults and review current TV guides.

● Ask the children to read the response from the BBC at the end of the letter and, in groups of four, make notes for a letter that could be written in reply. What do they think about the BBC's response? Is it good enough? Could it have been approached differently?

● Research the issue of sport on TV. Gather together a selection of television guides and tally up the level of sport coverage. Survey opinion within the school, collate comments from children, staff and parents, and let the children use these to prepare their own persuasive piece on the issue. Is there too much sport on TV? Are there people who feel very strongly in one particular direction? Does anyone really watch golf?

● Ask the children to write a letter to the BBC. It could be based on the notes constructed in shared writing (see above), following either point of view. The children may wish to focus their letter on a separate point (such as there's too much of the wrong sort of sport and not enough football).

Extension/further reading

Children could look through current television guides for examples of letters which are similar to this one, and judge the extent to which they agree or disagree with each of them.

5: 3: T12: to read and evaluate letters, e.g. from newspapers, magazines, intended to inform, protest, complain, persuade, considering (i) how they are set out (ii) how language is used, e.g. to gain attention, respect, manipulate

5: 3: T14: to select and evaluate a range of texts, in print or other media, for persuasiveness, clarity, quality of information

5: 3: T17: to draft and write individual, group or class letters for real purposes, e.g. put a point of view, comment on an emotive issue, protest; to edit and present to finished state

powerful words and phrases to grab reader's attention

states opinions

argument linked by connective moving to new point (the changing of schedules)

anticipates objections to point being made

Sport on TV

Once again TV's obsession with sport destroyed our choice of viewing (Saturday 13 April). Not content with five-and-a-quarter hours on BBC1, five hours 50 minutes on ITV and two hours ten minutes on Channel 4, BBC2 then took off its tribute to Billy Wilder and replaced it with Masters golf.

It may be a surprise to those making this decision, but there are licence-payers out here who have no interest in sport and feel entitled to an alternative.

I also object to the changing of published schedules, except when made necessary by vital breaking news or the need to meet other demands of national significance. Golf does not fall into those categories.

I dread this summer, with the usual Wimbledon, athletics and cricket being joined by World Cup soccer. Will there be anything for me to watch?

Jeffrey Butcher
Waltham Abbey, Essex
The BBC apologised for changing the schedule, but because rain had stopped play on the Friday, the second round had to be completed earlier the following day. As the BBC has the live rights to this coverage, it was obliged to broadcast the competition. Sunset Boulevard will be shown on 11 May.

letter giving an opinion has supporting factual detail

statement to persuade

letter ends with a rhetorical question (one not expecting an answer) which is used to emphasise point being made

5: 3: T15: from reading, to collect and investigate use of persuasive devices: e.g. words and phrases: e.g. *'surely', 'it wouldn't be very difficult...'*; persuasive definitions, e.g. *'no-one but a complete idiot...', 'every right-thinking person would ...' 'the real truth is...'*; rhetorical questions *'are we expected to..?' 'where will future audiences come from..?;*. pandering, condescension, concession etc.; *'Naturally, it takes time for local residents...*

5: 3: T19: to construct an argument in note form or full text to persuade others of a point of view and:
● present the case to the class or a group
● evaluate its effectiveness

Age of majority is not a minor matter

Background

Women have had the right to vote for less than a century. Suffrage can still be considered a contentious issue. The age of majority – the age at which an individual is deemed mature enough to vote – has settled at 18. However, there are a number of other responsibilities in life that can be taken on at 16, such as getting married, provided a parent's or guardian's permission has been obtained, or leaving school.

Shared reading and discussing the text

● Ask the children how much they know about elections. Ask them to make a few brief notes independently, listing some of the things they know about the subject. Write their main points on the board. Do they know what voting is for? Do they know who is allowed to vote? Some children may have visited a polling station with their parents. They may even have opinions as to who they would elect, and why.

● Read the text, asking the children to concentrate on the case that is being made and the arguments put forward in its favour. Once they have read it through, ask them to pick out the arguments that are made in favour of 16-year-olds voting. The three main points are: that 16-year-olds are entitled to other rights and responsibilities; that 16-year-olds can be affected by the legislation passed by those elected; and that there is a gap between the age at which they have the knowledge and education necessary to vote and the time when they are allowed to vote themselves (this may have the effect of making them uncommitted with regard to voting). Encourage the children to note the way in which opinions are stated as if they are irrefutable facts.

● Identify how the text connects things – voter apathy caused by the lack of young votes; voting as part of the teaching of citizenship yet the inability of young people to vote. Point out the way in which the words *yet* and *but* help to put forward the writer's reasoned case in this letter.

● Remove the text. Ask the children to recall how persuasive texts are structured (main point, arguments in favour of it, tackling of objection, final point). Once they have done this, ask them if they can recall the main point and the arguments made in this letter. A clear persuasive piece will be something the reader can recall after it has been taken away. Assess how effectively this one has been presented – that is, how much can they remember? Revisit the text to see what they have missed out.

Activities

● Ask the children to think of arguments against voting being lowered to 16. They may think the age is too young. Alternatively, they may want to ask why 16 should be the age – why not 15, or 11? Can they think of reasons for the writer arguing for the age to be 16? It might be worth pointing out that the writer omits the fact that many five-year-olds are affected by government policy, yet she doesn't argue for children in Reception classes to be able to vote.

● Encourage the children to canvass the opinions of others about when people should be able to vote. They could ask their parents or other members of staff – or they may know a 16-year-old whom they could 'interview'. Suggest that the children take notes to keep as a record.

● Ask the children to prepare a news report on this issue, working in small groups. They should present different sides of the argument, taking on the roles of questioners and questioned. The news report can then be presented, as in a news studio.

Extension/further reading

Children could read further material on the subject of elections. They could find out what MPs do and how often they are elected. How are new governments formed? This could be followed up by a request to the local MP to visit the class and answer questions on parliament and the voting system.

5: 3: T12: to read and evaluate letters, e.g. from newspapers, magazines, intended to inform, protest, complain, persuade, considering (i) how they are set out (ii) how language is used, e.g. to gain attention, respect, manipulate

5: 3: T14: to select and evaluate a range of texts, in print or other media, for persuasiveness, clarity, quality of information

opinion presented as fact

persuasive letters often respond to something, in this case an article

states the case, then follows it with 'because'

what campaign? (check back to 1st paragraph)

argument backed up with examples

Age of majority is not a minor matter

YOUR article on giving 16-year-olds the vote (*TES*, April 12) highlighted what we, the Liberal Democrat Youth and Students, are committed to.

We believe that this campaign is important because there are many injustices in the current British democracy. At present, 16-year-olds can get a full-time job and pay taxes, join the armed services, marry, and even have a family, yet they have no say over which government forms the policies which affect them and other issues important to them. For example, they are forced to accept a government that will introduce tuition fees and have no influence on how the education policy for their children will develop.

Sixteen-year-olds are both mature enough to vote and interested in helping to decide their government. Voter apathy among the young stems not from disinterest but from a belief that their views are being ignored.

While it might be argued that young people are insufficiently educated to vote we would point to the forthcoming introduction of citizenship teaching in schools.

Young people will be educated about how to vote and about other aspects of politics but then, once you have built up that knowledge and enthusiasm, there will be a two-year gap, until they reach 18, to put it into practice, which makes a farce of the situation.

Miranda Piercy
Chair, Liberal Democrat Youth and Students
4 Cowley Street
Westminster, London SW1

new paragraph for a new point (the nature of 16-year-olds)

connectives help to state argument clearly

explanation given in persuasive text: x causes y

use of persuasive words and phrases

5: 3: T15: from reading, to collect and investigate use of persuasive devices: e.g. words and phrases: e.g. *'surely', 'it wouldn't be very difficult...'*; persuasive definitions, e.g. *'no-one but a complete idiot...', 'every right-thinking person would ...' 'the real truth is...'*; rhetorical questions *'are we expected to..?' 'where will future audiences come from..?;.* pandering, condescension, concession etc.; *'Naturally, it takes time for local residents...*

5: 3: T19: to construct an argument in note form or full text to persuade others of a point of view and:
● present the case to the class or a group
● evaluate its effectiveness

edleader

Background

Unlike the format of a letter to a newspaper, an editorial is written by the newspaper. As a result, it will usually take a broader perspective and present various sides of an issue. It is important that a paper takes into account the breadth of opinion within the readership of its title. This editorial, from the magazine *Junior Education*, presents a response to a Government initiative – the policing of schools.

It is conventional for such editorials to remain anonymous as they represent the views of the publication as a whole.

Shared reading and discussing the text

● Read the text and ask the children to look for the initiative being discussed and the viewpoint expressed towards it. Pick out the way this is explored. The issue is presented, then points for and against it are aired. However, there is a leaning towards the idea that it might work. Unlike the two letters on pages 100 and 102, which state an opinion immediately, this text adopts a neutral stance until the sentence *But if the programme unfolds...* The alternative viewpoint is also presented (in the sentence immediately before it, *Many people will be asking themselves...*). Mark these two different points of view in the text.

● Why do the children think the opposing view has been presented? Establish that this has been done to present a balanced argument. Contrast this with the narrower viewpoints put forward in the texts on pages 100 and 102 (in which the children could insert their own text to present the argument from both sides).

● As arguments are developed and one point is linked with another, clauses are connected using commas or causal connectives. Ask the children to find examples, such as *But if the programme...*, *it will not only provide...*, and annotate the text. Can they pick out the verbs used and identify the clauses?

● Highlight the adjectives used in the text and the way they strengthen the point of view adopted (for example *valuable, enormous*).

● The final two sentences present opinions disguised as facts. Can the children spot the key words in the final sentence which tell us to be careful about whether they are facts? The words are *suggest* and *may*.

● How would the children respond to a school police service? Can they think of reasons why this could be a bad idea? Ask them to draw on their own reactions to this proposal, which will involve their own feelings about school, and weigh up their response.

Activities

● Ask the children to find words and phrases in the text that show how supportive the writer is towards the proposal. Ask them to annotate a copy, circling words and phrases that show the viewpoint of the writer (for example, *breaking down barriers, changing children's attitudes towards authority*).

● Working in a group, can the children write a response to the proposal as if they were the editorial board of a magazine? They will need to agree on the stance they are going to take and how they will present their perceived views of others regarding the proposal. (Remind them of the sentence beginning *Many people...* in the text here that brings in the thoughts of others.) After their conference, each child can write their own editorial, making sure that it reflects the views of the group.

● Using this text as a model, the children could write a persuasive commentary about an issue of their own choice. They should try to construct their own multiple-clause sentences, using language such as *If... then...* or *As... so...*, and include sentences in which they acknowledge other people's points of view, adding their own comments.

Extension/further reading

Ask the children to root through some recent tabloid newspapers to look at the editorial stances being taken on current events. They could collect similar examples from magazines and television guides.

5: 3: T13: to read other examples, e.g. newspaper comment, headlines, adverts, fliers. Compare writing which informs and persuades, considering, e.g.
● the deliberate use of ambiguity, half-truth, bias
● how opinion can be disguised to seem like fact

5: 3: T14: to select and evaluate a range of texts, in print or other media, for persuasiveness, clarity, quality of information

5: 3: S4: to use punctuation marks accurately in complex sentences

edleader

As part of its attempt to improve behaviour in schools, curb truancy and cut crime, the Government has announced that headteachers facing the toughest behavioural challenges – those in some inner city schools – will be offered the chance to have a police officer stationed in or around the school. Many people will be asking themselves how and why society has stooped so low that we need police patrols to maintain order in our schools and to ensure that pupils remain inside (and intruders remain outside) the perimeters of the school fence. But if the programme unfolds as the Government intends, it will not only provide valuable back-up for teachers, it should bring enormous benefits in terms of breaking down barriers, changing children's attitudes towards authority and building a sense of community in our inner cities. Pilot initiatives in London are certainly a testament to this. Early figures from a pilot scheme in Southwark schools suggest that a police presence may have reduced truancy-related crime in the area by as much as 95 per cent.

presents the issue to be discussed

acknowledges the views of others

comma marks boundary between 2 clauses

responds with own viewpoint

gives points in favour of the issue

adjectives strengthen opinion being given

opinion presented as fact

opinion supported with factual material, but caution may be required – how factual is it?

5: 3: T15: from reading, to collect and investigate use of persuasive devices: e.g. words and phrases: e.g. *'surely', 'it wouldn't be very difficult…';* persuasive definitions, e.g. *'no-one but a complete idiot…', 'every right-thinking person would …' 'the real truth is…';* rhetorical questions *'are we expected to..?' 'where will future audiences come from..?;.* pandering, condescension, concession etc.; *'Naturally, it takes time for local residents…* deliberate ambiguities, e.g. *'probably the best…in the world' 'known to cure all…', 'the professionals' choice'*

5: 3: S6: to investigate clauses through:
● identifying the main clause in a long sentence
● investigating sentences which contain more than one clause
● understanding how clauses are connected (e.g. by combining three short sentences into one)

Dictionary definitions

Extracts 1, 2 and 3

Background

This text comprises three different groups of dictionary entries, each one starting with the word *cult*. The first group of entries has been taken from a school dictionary aimed at Years 5 and 6, the second from a modern copy of Chambers dictionary and the third from a Chambers dictionary from the early part of the last century (1901). Placing the three sets of entries together provides the children with the opportunity to look at features common to dictionaries, including the entry, how the word should be pronounced, the definitions and examples of use. The contrast can also be seen between the different entries made at different times and for various audiences.

Shared reading and discussing the text

● Write the words *cult, cultivated* and *culture* on the board and ask the children if they have any ideas about how these words are pronounced and their meanings. Can they also give examples of how each word could be used? (If they have read the Tao text, see page 94, they will have encountered at least one of these words before.) Use the children's responses to make notes around the words on the board. Now look up the words in a dictionary to see how close the children were to the definitions.

● Read through the first extract from the school dictionary, pointing out the headword (*cult*) followed by the information about the way in which the word is spoken (*say* kult), the definitions (two in this case) and the sample phrase showing how the word can be used. Having looked at these different elements, find them in the entry for *cultivate*. Now look at the extracts from the other two dictionaries and ask the children if they can see the same features (headword, how the word is pronounced, definition and sample phrase).

● Look at the range of dictionaries on this page. Ask the children if they have any thoughts about who the audience would be for each text. Which text do they think is the oldest? Which one do they think is aimed at a younger audience? Why do they think one dictionary has words that aren't in another? Point out the older words in the Chambers 1901 dictionary, including *culter* and *cultism*.

Activities

● Explore the connections between the entries. Each of these words can be traced back to the word *cult* and in the entries the Latin root *colere* (to till, to worship) can be found. Can the children see how attending to something, spending time on it and turning it over (cultivation) can be linked to thinking about belief and reflecting on it (worship)? Ask the children to write down any connections they think can be made between all the words that are defined.

● Working in pairs, the children could try devising some sentences that include the dictionary words, showing their correct meanings.

● Ask the children to look at the dictionary entries to make their own evaluation of the range of texts. Which group of entries do they find easiest to read and understand? How is the amount of information available balanced against ease of access to the text? Giving the children copies of the text, ask them to cut out the three groups of entries and paste them onto a separate sheet of paper in order of preference. One way of deciding this could be to ask themselves which dictionary they would use again.

Extension/further reading

Children can further investigate how words can be formed from root words, looking through dictionaries. Start them off by giving them a short word, such as *play* or *book*, and asking them to find examples of words that have connections with it (*playful, bookworm* and so on).

5: 3: W11: to use a range of dictionaries and understand their purposes, e.g. dictionaries of slang, phrases, idioms, contemporary usage, synonyms, antonyms, quotations and thesauruses

5: 3: W12: to use dictionaries efficiently to explore spellings, meanings, derivations, e.g. by using alphabetical order, abbreviations, definitions with understanding

Dictionary definitions

structure of entry:

headword

pronunciation

meanings

example of how to use the word

❶

cult (*say* kult) *noun*
1 a religion **2** a thing or person that is popular only with a small group of people: *a cult film*

cultivate (*say* **kul**-ti-vate) *verb*
1 to prepare and work land in order to plant and raise crops **2** to make something stronger and better: *to cultivate friendships*

Word Family: cultivation *noun*
Similar Meaning: for definition 1 **till**

cultivated (*say* **kul**-ti-vay-ted) *adjective*
1 produced by or using cultivation: *cultivated land* **2** well-educated and well-behaved

culture (*say* **kul**-cher) *noun*
1 the ideas, knowledge and beliefs of a particular society or group of people: *Aboriginal culture* **2** art, literature, music and so on

root word

root word leads to new words

❷

cult *kult*, *n.* **1** a system of religious belief. **2** a sect. **3** great devotion to: *the cult of physical fitness.*
[Same root as **cultivate**.]

cultivate *kul'ti-vāt*, *v.t.* **1** to till or prepare (ground) for crops. **2** to grow (a crop). **3** to develop, or improve, by care or study: *to cultivate good manners.* **4** to encourage (e.g. science, friendship). **5** to seek the company of (a person).

cultiva'tion *n.* **1** the art or practice of cultivating. **2** a refined, cultivated state.

cul'tivator *n.* an implement for breaking up ground, esp. among crops.

culture *kul'chir*, *n.* **1** cultivation. **2** educated refinement. **3** a type of civilisation: *Bronze Age culture.*

cul'tural *adj.* **cul'turally** *adv.*

cul'tured *adj.* **1** cultivated. **2** well educated, refined.
[L. *colêre, cultum*, to till, worship.]

❸

Cult, kult, *n.* a system of religious belief, worship. — also **Cult'us**.
[L. *cultus—colĕre*, to worship.]

Culter, kul'tér, *n.* obsolete form of **Coulter**. —*adjs.* **Cultiros'tral, Culturos'tral; Cul'trate, -d,** shaped like a pruning-knife; **Cul'triform,** in the form of a pruning-knife: sharp-edged.

Cultism, kult'ism, *n.* a style of writing after the manner of Luis de Góngora y Argote (1561–1627), a Spanish lyric poet— *estilo culto*, being florid, pedantic, often obscure (see **Gongorism**). —*ns.* **Cult'ist, Cult'erist**. [Sp. *culte*, elegant—L. *cultus*.]

Cultivate, kul'ti-vāt, *v.t.* to till or produce by tillage: to prepare for crops: to devote attention to: to civilise or refine.—*adjs.* **Cul'tivable, Cultivat'able,** capable of being cultivated.—*ns.* **Cultivā'tion,** the art or practice of cultivating: civilisation: refinement; **Cul'tivator.— Cultivate** a person's friendship, to endeavour to get his good-will. [Low L. *cultivāre, -ātum*—L. *colĕre*, to till, to worship.]

Culture, kul'tûr, *n.* cultivation: the state of being cultivated: refinement the result of cultivation.—*v.t.* to cultivate: to improve.—*adjs.* **Cul'turable; Cul'tural.**—*p. adj.* **Cul'tured,** cultivated: well educated: refined.—*adj.* **Cul'tureless**. [L. *cultūra—colĕre*.]

Cultus. See Cult.

Latin root connected to meaning of word today

word from an older dictionary; word no longer in use

5: 3: T14: to select and evaluate a range of texts, in print or other media, for persuasiveness, clarity, quality of information

5: 3: S2: to understand how writing can be adapted for different audiences and purposes, e.g. by changing vocabulary and sentence structures

Thesaurus entries *Extracts 1 and 2*

Background

A thesaurus draws together a selection of words that possess a similar meaning to the headword. In addition to providing synonyms, thesauruses group words into related concepts and, in this sense, they are like dictionaries going backwards: in a dictionary the reader starts with a word and looks it up to find the meaning; in a thesaurus the reader usually starts with a word and its meaning and looks it up to find another word. Some thesauruses are organised into themes and families of words, others are organised alphabetically. The school thesauruses used here are both examples of the latter, though one is far more detailed than the other.

One point to watch when children are using a thesaurus is that they can fall into the trap of adopting an alternative word by just slotting it into the space vacated by the initial one. They start with a sentence like *I decided to scale the wall* and find the word *escalate* given as a thesaurus entry, so end up writing *I decided to escalate the wall*. A way round this is to encourage children to use a thesaurus as a way of seeking out words they already know, as a reminder rather than simply to find new words. When children do want to use words with which they were previously unfamiliar they should use a thesaurus in conjunction with a dictionary.

Shared reading and discussing the text

● List the words *say, scarce* and *scare* (taken from extract 1) on the board and ask the children if, for each word, they can think of other words that mean the same. As they offer you examples, ask them if they can place the words in context, giving an example in each case of how the alternative word could be used (for *scare*, they might say *terrify*, adding an example such as *I didn't mean to terrify you*).

● Look at the shorter thesaurus entries (extract 2) and encourage the children to try out the words listed by using them in sentences of their own. Remind them to make sure that they use the words appropriately, so that each sentence retains its sense.

● Returning to extract 1, the children will notice that each headword is followed by its part of speech. Can the children think of ways in which an initial word (for example, *scare*) can be transformed to make other words which are different parts of speech (for example, *scary*)? Ask them to check whether their secondary words have been listed here.

Activities

● Ask the children to look for examples in extract 1 of words that can be changed in accordance with the spelling rule that words ending in modifying *e* drop *e* when adding *ing* – *scale* becomes *scaling; scare* becomes *scaring*. Can they also find words which can be grouped together to demonstrate the use of spelling rules they know? For example, under the word *scan* each sentence gives the word *scanned*, changing the present tense *scan* to the past tense *scanned*. They can then move on to words that are not given after the headword but can be linked to it, for example *unscarred* is the opposite of *scarred* under *scar* (demonstrating negation); *scantier* and *scantiest* are the comparative and superlative forms of the adjective *scanty*.

● Children can play with the thesaurus entries by trying to write a paragraph that uses as many of them as possible. You can set the parameters for this game – their paragraph has to be a letter, it has to be about events that took place in a supermarket, and so on.

● Ask the children to make a new thesaurus in which they compile their own entries. This can be done as a poster made for children in a younger class, providing them with alternative words to use in place of ones they are currently focusing on (for example, different words for *walk: go, step, stride…*). Alternatively, the children could devise a thesaurus that uses a range of words in common use in their own family or among their friends – *waffle, gab, yak* (for *say*), or *blag, chin chin* (for *lie*), or *wicked, sound, cool* (for *good*), for example. This will also help them to develop their awareness of dialect.

Thesaurus entries

❶

spelling changes, turning verb ('say') to noun ('saying')

say *verb*
1 *Colin tried to say what he really thought.* ▶ to state, to express, to convey, to explain
2 *I said that it was getting late.* ▶ to mention, to remark, to comment
3 *She was too angry to say his name.* ▶ to speak, to utter

saying *noun*
There is a saying that an apple a day keeps the doctor away. ▶ a proverb, an adage, a maxim, a motto, a slogan

scale *verb*
The climbers began to scale the rock face. ▶ to climb, to ascend, to mount

scales *plural noun*
The cat was too heavy to weigh in the scales. ▶ a balance

past tense form of 'scan'

scamper *verb*
You could hear the mice scampering back into their holes. ▶ to scurry, to scuttle, to dash, to hurry, to run

scan *verb*
1 *We scanned the landscape for signs of a road.* ▶ to study, to survey, to view, to gaze at, to scrutinize, to examine
2 *She scanned the book for a picture of the village.* ▶ to look through, to glance through, to skim, to read quickly

the pitfall of using what is listed in an automatic way – alternative words cover a wide field and need to be used carefully (a sensation is very different from an embarrassment)

scandal *noun*
1 *Their behaviour caused quite a scandal.* ▶ a sensation, an outrage, an embarrassment
2 *The newspaper article was full of scandal.* ▶ gossip, rumour

scandalous *adjective*
Their behaviour had not just been embarrassing but downright scandalous. ▶ disgraceful, outrageous, shameful, shocking

headword

scanty *adjective*
The furniture in the house was old and scanty. ▶ sparse, meagre, inadequate

part of speech

scar *noun*
The man had a scar on his left cheek. ▶ a mark, a blemish

example sentence showing a way in which the word can be used

scar *verb*
His face had been scarred in an accident. ▶ to mark, to disfigure, to damage

alternative words

scarce *adjective*
Fresh fruit was scarce because of the war. ▶ short, in short supply, lacking, sparse, meagre, limited, scanty

scarcely *adverb*
Donna had scarcely finished eating when the phone rang. ▶ barely, hardly, only just

scare *verb*
The noise was scaring the animals. ▶ to frighten, to alarm, to startle, to terrify

scare *noun*
You gave me quite a scare. ▶ a fright, a shock

scary *adjective*
(informal) *It was scary in the dark.* ▶ creepy, eerie, frightening, ghostly, spooky, uncanny, weird

❷

say	*v*	tell, state, declare, speak, express
scarce	*adj*	rare, short, few, uncommon

no example sentences given, just alternative words

simplified thesaurus – there are words missing here that are in the other extract ('saying' to 'scar')

part of speech

X30

Krindlekrax

It was the day for choosing a hero.

All the week before, Ruskin Splinter's school – St George's – had been casting its end-of-year play and only the role of hero remained. Ruskin wanted to play this part more than anything. "I was born to be a hero," he had told his teacher, Mr Lace. "Don't you think so?"

"I'm not sure," Mr Lace had replied, sucking a pencil. "We'll decide next Monday."

And now it was the day for deciding.

As soon as Ruskin woke up he stared at the photographs of famous actors that were stuck on his walls (Ruskin wanted to be a famous actor when he grew up) and started rehearsing lines from the play.

"I am brave and wise and wonderful," Ruskin said, getting dressed and going to the bathroom to clean his teeth.

He looked at his reflection in the mirror above the sink.

"What a hero you are!" he said to himself, the toothpaste frothing in his mouth.

Ruskin was eleven years old, extremely thin, with a bush of frizzy red hair. He wore green shorts that showed off his knobbly knees, green (lace-up) shoes that were too big for him ("You'll grow into them!" his mum had told him), a striped (green and white) T-shirt that made his arms look like twigs, and glasses with lenses so thick his eyes appeared the size of saucers.

When Ruskin had cleaned his teeth, he looked out of the bathroom window.

"Good morning, Lizard Street," he said in his squeaky whisper of a voice.

Philip Ridley

Story openings

SNATCHERS

Helen Cresswell

BEFORE YOU BEGIN…

Listen, I have a story to tell. It's mad and sad in parts and beautiful as well. Most stories have a time and a place. They happen because a particular person was in a particular place at a particular time. Think about it. If Wendy Darling had not lived in a certain tall house in a certain street in London, we should never have known the story of Peter Pan.

The particular person in this story is called Ellie. But I don't know when it happened, or where.

STEP BY WICKED STEP

Anne Fine

Even before they reached the haunted house, the night had turned wild. The face of the minibus driver flickered from blue to white under the lightning. Each peal of thunder made the map in Mr Plumley's hand shiver. And the five leftover pupils from Stagfire School peered anxiously through the rain-spattered windows into the storm and the black night.

"There!"

"Where?"

"Over there. See? Up that overgrown driveway."

THE LOTTIE PROJECT

Jacqueline Wilson

SCHOOL

I knew exactly who I was going to sit next to in class. Easy-peasy, simple-pimple. It was going to be Angela, with Lisa sitting at the nearest table to us. I'm never quite sure if I like Lisa or Angela best, so it's only fair to take turns.

Jo said what if Angela and Lisa want to sit together with *you* behind or in front or at the side.

In the sewer: Krindlekrax

It was cold in the sewer and full of echoing sounds that made his eardrums ring.

Suddenly, Ruskin saw the walking stick.

It was floating in the water.

The current was carrying it along, deeper and deeper into the heart of the sewer.

Ruskin ran until he was alongside the stick, then got to his knees and reached out.

He stretched as far as he could.

His fingers had just touched the walking stick when the current carried it off again.

Ruskin jumped up and followed.

He was breathing very hard now and – despite being cold – he was sweating.

The torchlight flickered over walls and across the water.

Corky was right, Ruskin thought. It *is* beautiful down here.

The green of the slime sparkled like emeralds and the water was satin smooth.

The walking stick stopped moving.

It had got attached to some particularly thick slime.

Ruskin rushed up, got to his knees and reached out.

His fingertips grazed across the surface of the water.

He grabbed hold of the walking stick.

"Got it!" he said.

And that's when he realized.

It wasn't slime the stick was attached to.

It was rats!

Philip Ridley

The Gizmo

The tramp disappears around a corner. By the time I turn it he is nowhere to be seen. The street is full of people who are coming out of a church. It is a wedding and all the people are dressed in their best clothes and throwing confetti.

"He is hiding," I say to myself. "The tramp is hiding in the crowd." I start to push through the people, trying to find the tramp.

"Go away," sniffs a lady as I push past her legs. "Dreadful boy. Smelly. Awful. How dare you dress like that at a wedding. Go away."

I pretend not to hear. I have to get my clothes back or Dad will kill me. Suddenly I find myself staring at the bride. She is beautiful. Lovely. Nearly as good as my girlfriend Kate. She wears a veil in her hair. And flowers. And a long white dress.

Two little kids in purple are holding a long train out at the back. Her new husband is standing next to her, all dressed up to kill. I recognise him. He is the coach of our local football team. At the back is the preacher. His head nearly falls off when he sees me and my outfit.

The bride looks at me. And I look at her. She is shocked to see a boy dressed like a tramp.

Suddenly there is a hum. It is coming from my pocket. "No, no, please no," I scream. The crowd are all looking at me. Everyone falls silent. The gizmo beeps.

And the bride is dressed like a tramp.

And I am dressed like a bride.

She opens her mouth and screams in horror. I open my mouth and scream in horror.

Talk About Short

HE WAS ALONE, and in the dark; and when he reached out for the matches, the matches were put into his hand.

Kevin Crossley-Holland

No-Speaks

I am the child who stopped talking
Three years ago. There was heavy snow.
It was a blow to my family, I know.
They call me No-Speaks.
It has been one hundred and fifty-six weeks
Since I came to my decision about speech.
I clocked it was a waste of time,
to talk in plain speech or rhyme.
So, I watch the telling hands chime.
I watch the trees grow big beards, fuzzy hair.
Then, I watch them get alopecia.
I watch the snow melt into summer.
I hold my tongue round the clock.
They call me No-Speaks.
I shut my mouth from season to season.
I have a very good reason,
For never saying a single word.
Not a single dickie bird.
(I was not struck by lightning.
I did not witness something shocking.)
(If two people tell the same lie
at the same time, one will die
Before the year is over.)
My lips are sealed, January to December.
They call me No-Speaks.

Jackie Kay

The New Poem (for 18 words)

New words
Should be used to being
Where they have not yet got.
So this is the poem.

This poem is the words,
So new, have yet
Not got used to being.
Where should they be?

This poem is so new
The words have not yet
Got used to being
Where they should be.

Roger McGough

SKY DAY DREAM

WITH THEM

COULD FLY OFF

I WISHED THAT I

INTO THE SKY

FLY OFF

SOME CROWS

ONCE I SAW

Robert Froman

HOMEWEB

A COBWEB MAY LOOK MESSY

BUT TO SOME SPI-DER IT IS HOME

Robert Froman

If the Earth

If   the   Earth
were only a few feet in diameter,
floating a few feet above a field somewhere,
people would come from everywhere to marvel
at it. People would walk around it, marvelling at its
big pools of water, its little pools and the water flowing
between the pools. People would marvel at the bumps on
it, and the holes in it, and they would marvel at the very thin
layer of gas surrounding it and the water suspended in the gas.
The people would marvel at all the creatures walking around
the surface of the ball, and at the creatures in the water. The
people would declare it as sacred because it was the only one,
and they would protect it so that it would not be hurt. The
ball would be the greatest wonder known, and people would
come to pray to it, to be healed, to gain knowledge, to know
beauty and to wonder how it could be. People would
love it, and defend it with their lives because they
would somehow know that their lives, their own
roundness, could be nothing without it. If
the Earth were only a few feet in
diameter.

Joe Miller

MARTIAN MAMA

Blackout Sketch

Characters
MARTIAN MAMA

MARTIAN JUNIOR

Setting the Stage

The only essential part of the costume is an extra set of arms pinned under Mama's regular arms. You can make these arms from sleeves of old clothes stuffed with newspaper.

> **Note:** *This sketch can be changed easily to suit any kind of alien or monster. Just change the names of the foods.*

SCENE. MAMA *is washing dishes, with her back turned to the audience.* JUNIOR *is sitting in a high chair eating dinner. The audience can't see Mama's extra arms because her back is turned.*

JUNIOR. Mama, I want something to drink! Gimme something to drink! (*He pounds his fists on his tray.*)

MAMA. I just did, Junior. It's right in front of you, dear.

JUNIOR (*picks up a glass of green-coloured water*). Gimme some moon-cheese pie, and more asteroid pudding, too. Come on, gimme it!

MAMA. Just a minute. Can't you see I'm busy with these dishes?

JUNIOR (*throws his water on the floor*). Uh-oh, Mama, my comet juice spilled. Hurry, clean it up! Mama, I want my dessert! Gimme my dessert!

MAMA (*turns around, revealing her four arms*). I can't do everything! I only have four arms!

BLACKOUT

Terry Halligan

Krindlekrax playscript

Scene Three

RUSKIN'S KITCHEN

Sunlight illuminates cooker, fridge, chairs and table. A football lies in the middle of table and has obviously smashed much cutlery (including many plates of toast) and knocked toaster to the floor.

Wendy Splinter is picking up toaster. She is thirty-three years old and wearing a (faded 'n' frayed) green dressing gown, fluffy green slippers and round rimmed spectacles. She is pale, thin and has frizzy, red hair.

Winston Splinter, her husband, is huddled beside the cooker, trembling with fear. He is thirty-five years old and is wearing (green and white) pyjama bottoms, string vest, green socks and round rimmed spectacles. He is pale, thin and balding (what hair remains is frizzy and red).

Wendy   Look at the mess! If the toaster's damaged… well, we can't afford a new one, you know.

Winston   Not my fault.

Wendy   Someone's got to do something about Elvis.

Puts bread in toaster.

We'll have no windows left at this rate.

Ruskin enters, now wearing green shorts, a striped (green and white) T-shirt and green, lace-up shoes. He is clutching satchel, sword and shield.

Ruskin   Morning, Mum.

Kisses Wendy.

Wendy   Mind where you tread! Elvis is up to his tricks again.

Ruskin   So I see. Morning, Dad.

Winston   Not my fault.

Ruskin   Well… today's the day, everyone.

Removes broken crockery from seat and sits.

Wendy   Tea?

Pours cup of tea for Ruskin.

Ruskin   I've learnt all my lines.

Wendy   That's the third window we've lost this month, Winston! I'm still finding glass in the living room. And as for the bathroom… well, no privacy there!

Winston   Not my fault.

Takes can of lager from fridge.

DEAR BRUTUS

PURDIE. Tell them what you told us, Lob.

LOB (*with a pout for the credulous*). It is all nonsense, of course; just foolish talk of the villagers. They say that on Midsummer Eve there is a strange wood in this part of the country.

ALICE (*lowering*). Where?

PURDIE. Ah, that is one of its most charming features. It is never twice in the same place apparently. It has been seen on different parts of the Downs and on More Common; once it was close to Radley village and another time about a mile from the sea. Oh, a sporting wood!

LADY CAROLINE. And Lob is anxious that we should all go and look for it?

COADE. Not he; Lob is the only sceptic in the house. Says it is all rubbish, and that we shall be sillies if we go. But we believe, eh, Purdie?

PURDIE (*waggishly*). Rather!

LOB (*the artful*). Just wasting the evening. Let us have a round game at cards here instead.

PURDIE (*grandly*). No, sir, I am going to find that wood.

JOANNA. What is the good of it when it is found?

PURDIE. We shall wander in it deliciously, listening to a new sort of bird called the Philomel.

(LOB *is behaving in the most exemplary manner; making sweet little clucking sounds.*)

JOANNA (*doubtfully*). Shall we keep together, Mr. Purdie?

PURDIE. No, we must hunt in pairs.

JOANNA (*converted*). I think it would be rather fun.

JM Barrie

A Little Bit
From the Author

I have only stolen something once in my life. I was six years old and I took a packet of hair pins from the lounge-room of the lady next door. They would have been worth about twenty cents, I guess.

That type of hair pin was only used by girls and women so I gave them to my mother. I also told a lie. I said, "Look what I found on the footpath, Mum."

Well, she was so pleased. "Oh, you are a good boy," she said. "That's just what I need." She went on and on and on about how clever and kind I was. The more she said the worse I felt. My conscience really gave me a bad time. The thought that I had done something wrong just wouldn't go away and it made me unhappy for ages. I was a thief. I felt so bad that I have never forgotten the incident.

When I was a teacher some of my students were talked into stealing a hosepipe by some big boys. They didn't know what to do with the hosepipe and in the end they threw it in a pond. Someone saw them and came and reported it to the school. They had to buy a new hosepipe and say sorry to the owner.

Both of these things happened a long time ago. But last year I got to thinking about a guilty conscience. And how some people talk other people into stealing. It seemed like good material for a book.

So I wrote a book called *The Gizmo* about a boy who steals a gadget from the market. He throws it away but it follows him around. Like a guilty conscience.

These little events are the stuff of stories. I am always on the lookout for them.

Paul Jennings

Willy the Warthog

One of the most disastrous school talks of all time was given by American Lawrence Bilbo, whose lecture on 'Why We Shouldn't be Cruel to Animals' culminated in him being shot in the buttock by a belligerent caretaker. An ardent animal rights campaigner, Mr Bilbo, 36, travelled the length and breadth of America giving talks to schoolchildren on animal welfare. "I used to dress up as Willy the Warthog," explained the caring conservationist. "I had a furry brown costume, and tusks, and little trotters that I wore over my shoes like galoshes. It gave the whole lecture a bit of topicality and the children loved it." On the day in question, Mr Bilbo had arrived to give a talk at a school in Cruger, Mississippi, secreting himself in the toilet and donning his Willy the Warthog costume before scampering into the corridor with a loud snort, ready to address the school's 200 children. Unfortunately, he was spotted by short-sighted caretaker Albert Miggins, who, convinced he was actually 'a lion or something', fetched his shotgun and pursued a terrified Mr Bilbo into the school playground, where he shot him in the backside. The lacerated lecturer has since discarded his warthog costume in favour of a bright-orange three-piece suit. "It's safer that way," he explained.

Paul Sussman

Unhappy ending for the newborn hippo rescued from a lake

Exhausted: The baby hippo perched at the side of the water

THE newborn hippo rescued from a rain-swollen lake has died, despite the best efforts of its mother and the fire brigade.

The 18in high calf was delivered on a ledge at the side of the lake by its mother, Bar-Bel, but kept slipping into the water.

Bar-Bel desperately tried to nudge her baby to safety. When she failed, the keepers at West Midlands Safari Park called in the fire brigade.

They pumped 200,000 gallons from the lake and scooped the little hippo up in a net. The animal was then given oxygen and put under a heat lamp as it fought for life.

Yesterday, however, head warden Bob Lawrence announced that the 50lb baby had died 'in its sleep' having swallowed a large amount of water during the rescue.

"We are all very, very disappointed but the calf was just too exhausted after her ordeal," he said.

"Everything humanly possible was done to save the calf and the fire brigade did a magnificent job."

Text © The Daily Mail. Photograph © News Team International

Driver and Vehicle
Licensing Agency

INS116R

Don't be a REJECT!

Many photocard applications are being rejected.

To ensure this does not happen to your application, you need to:

- return either your current passport or your birth certificate, copies of these are unacceptable (see Section 4 on the application form)

- make sure the photograph is **acceptable** and is signed on the **back** (see Sections 5 and 7)

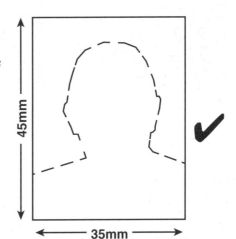

45mm

35mm

- sign in black within the **white box** (see Section 8)

An executive agency of the
Department of the Environment,
Transport and the Regions

NB This leaflet has been updated. For current information, visit www.dvla.gov.uk/drivers/photocard_licences.htm

30

Your short story

Here are some tips for planning your short story.

Plan your beginning and your ending and the bridge between the two.

- Plan your story so you know where you will be in 45 minutes.
- Plan a strong middle, bridging the beginning and the end.

Make your characters workable, interesting and enjoyable.

- Stick to two or three characters we will know and enjoy.
- Name and describe your characters.

Let the reader know where they are.

- Sense a setting (what does it look, sound and smell like?) and take your reader there.
- Use adjectives to describe the place.

Plan some dialogue.

- Use it to tell what happens in the story (for example, "The door is opening!").
- Use interesting words for "said".

Think through the thoughts and feelings.

- Let readers feel what a character feels.
- Give your characters an 'inner voice' (words that tell what we wouldn't see, for example "I realised…", "Lou was afraid that…").

36

Pick a Book

You need 9 books for this trick and a willing assistant.

1. Arrange the books on the floor in 3 rows of 3.

2. Say to your audience, "While I am out of the room, choose a book. Then I'll come back and tell you which one it is."

3. Leave the room while the book is being chosen, and then return.

4. Watch your assistant. He will point at a book which has NOT been chosen and say, "Is this the book?" You say no. But look very carefully at where his finger is pointing. Imagine the front of the book is divided into 3 rows of 3, just like the books. If he is pointing to the middle of the book, for example, it means they have chosen the middle book. And so on.

5. Now you know which is the right book. Your assistant will carry on pointing to books and you will know whether to say yes or no.

Alan Snow and Louise Cook (Walker Books)

THE CREATION

In the beginning the black waters of Nun enveloped everything and there was darkness and silence everywhere. Then suddenly, out of the watery depths, the pointed tips of a closed lotus flower and a primeval mound appeared. Slowly, they both rose above the water until they were fully formed. The lotus flower then began to uncurl its tightly closed petals and a brilliant yellow light shone from it. When fully open it revealed the small, but perfectly formed figure of the creator, Amun-Ra, sitting in the blaze of light, surrounded by a wonderful perfume. He then turned into a beautiful phoenix bird and flew to the newly formed mound which was shaped like a pyramid. He settled down there stretching out his brightly coloured red and gold wings and gave a great cry which echoed in the silence around him.

Amun-Ra became lonely in his watery solitude and so, out of himself, he created a son, Shu, the god of air, and a daughter, the lioness-headed Tefnut, goddess of the dew and of moisture. Amun-Ra was so proud of his children that he wept with happiness.

Shu and Tefnut then conceived a son, Geb, the earth god, and a daughter, Nut, the goddess of the sky. Geb and Nut cared deeply for each other and out of their love came four children. The first was a kind and honourable son, Osiris, who was followed by his brother, Seth. Lastly, Nut gave birth to two daughters, the brave and magical Isis, and her gentle and caring sister, Nephthys. These children, unlike their ancestors, lived on earth. After them many more gods and goddesses were born.

Lastly, Amun-Ra ordered the ram-headed god, Khnum, to turn his potter's wheel and fashion man out of clay. Gently breathing life into man, Amun-Ra now realized that he required a place to live, and so he created Egypt. Just as Amun-Ra had emerged from the waters of Nun, so he created the River Nile so that Egypt and its peoples could grow and prosper.

Sarah Quie

The Hunting of Death

A MYTH FROM RWANDA

The angel huntsmen were close to his heels when Death came to a field, where an old lady was digging.

"Oh glorious, lovely creature!" panted Death. "I have run many miles across this hard world, but never have I seen such a beauty as you! Surely my eyes were made for looking at you. Let me sit here on the ground and gaze at you!"

The old lady giggled. "Ooooh! What a flatterer you are, little crinkly one!"

"Not at all! I'd talk to your father at once and ask to marry you, but a pack of hunters is hard on my heels!"

"I know, I heard God say," said the old woman. "You must be that Death he talked of."

"But *you* wouldn't like me to be killed, would you – a woman of your sweet nature and gentle heart? A maiden as lovely as you would never wish harm on a poor defenceless creature!" The drum beats came closer and closer.

The old woman simpered. "Oh well. Best come on in under here," she said and lifted her skirt, showing a pair of knobbly knee-caps. In out of the sunlight scuttled Death, and twined himself, thin and sinuous, round her legs.

The angel huntsmen came combing the land, the line of them stretching from one horizon to the other. "Have you seen Death pass this way?"

"Not I," answered the old lady, and they passed on, searching the corn ricks, burning the long grass, peering down the wells. Of course, they found no trace of Death.

Out he came from under her skirts, and away he ran without a backward glance. The old woman threw a rock after him, and howled, "Come back! Stop that rascal, God! Don't let him get away! He said he'd marry me!"

But God was angry. "You sheltered Death from me when I hunted him. Now I shan't shelter you from him when he comes hunting for your heartbeat!" And with that he recalled his angel huntsmen to Heaven.

Geraldine McCaughrean

Orpheus and Eurydice

As the boat glided across the river, a dark shape loomed up, then a terrible barking split the air. It was Cerberus, the three-headed guard dog. Orpheus took his lyre on to his lap and began to play. He played a song without words, and the ferryman stopped splashing his oars to listen. The barking sank to a yelp, then to a whimper. When the boat touched shore, Orpheus stepped out of the boat, still playing.

Throughout the Underworld, the souls of the Dead stopped to listen. Pluto, King of the Dead, also listened. "What's that noise, wife?"

His wife, Persephone, knew at once, "It must be Orpheus the musician! Oh, if he is dead and his spirit is ours to keep, we shall have better music here than on earth!"

"Never! Music is forbidden here!" exclaimed Pluto.

At the sight of Orpheus – a man still wearing his earthly body – Pluto jumped up and pointed an angry finger. "You'll be sorry you dared to sneak down here, young man!"

Orpheus simply began to sing. He sang of Eurydice's beauty. He sang of their love. He sang of the spiteful snake and his unbearable loneliness. When the song finished, Pluto sank back into his throne, his hands over his face, and tears running down into his beard.

"Every time someone dies, there are people who want them alive again," said Pluto. "But you are the only one who ever made me allow this to happen. Eurydice shall return to the earth."

He clapped his hands, and feet could be heard running down a long corridor: the footsteps of Eurydice.

Orpheus peered through the gloom for a first glimpse of her dear face.

"If—" said Pluto.

"If?"

"If you can climb back to the sunlight without once turning to look at her face." He laughed unkindly.

Back Orpheus went towards the River Styx, and the swish of a woman's robes followed him. But he did not look back. Again Orpheus began to play. Again the great dog Cerberus lolled with delight and let him pass, licking him with three tongues. But Orpheus did not look back. Into the rowing boat he stepped, and someone stepped in behind him. The ferryman rowed two passengers across the river.

One last long climb and they would be free of the Underworld! Then Orpheus would be able to take Eurydice in his arms and kiss her and laugh about the dreary Kingdom of the Dead. "Not long now!" he called to her.

Why did Eurydice not reply? Perhaps Pluto had tricked him. Perhaps it was someone else following him. Or perhaps Eurydice had changed during her time in the Underworld, and didn't love her husband any more! Just as the first rays of sunlight came into view, Orpheus glanced quickly over his shoulder – just to be sure.

Oh yes, it was Eurydice. Those eyes, that hair, that sweet mouth calling his name: *Orpheus!*

She sank down like a drowning swimmer: "Orpheus, why?" She fell back down and the darkness swallowed her up.

"Eurydice!"

But she was gone. Orpheus had lost his beloved a second time.

Geraldine McCaughrean

HARE, HIPPO AND ELEPHANT

Hare was a lazy thing and when he got married and settled down he couldn't be bothered to get down to hard work. Go out and work in the fields so he could feed his wife and himself? Not on your life.

Then one day he had an idea.

He took a long rope and went into the forest to find Hippo.

"Uncle, will you listen to me a moment? Why don't we have a game here. I tie this rope to you, and I'll see if I can pull you out of the mud."

"Right," said Hippo, "sounds like a great game to me. I can't lose."

"Good," said Hare, "so I'll go off among the trees over there. The moment you feel a tug on the rope, you pull like mad, OK? But I'm warning you, I'm pretty strong."

Hippo laughed. "Yes, of course you are, Hare."

Hare tied the rope round Hippo and then went off among the trees and waited. It wasn't long before Elephant came down to the water-hole.

Hare stopped him. "Oh, uncle, have you got a moment? I'm looking for someone who wants a tug-of-war. Everyone I have a go with, I beat. What do you say?"

"Out of my way, little fool. I haven't got time to play silly games."

"No listen, uncle, I tell you what, if you win, I'll do anything you want.

I'll be your servant, I'll fetch and carry, anything."

Elephant liked the sound of that very much indeed. So he let Hare tie the rope round him and off went Hare, telling Elephant to start pulling when he felt a tug on the rope.

Half-way along the rope where neither Hippo nor Elephant could see him, Hare gave a tug on the rope, first one way and then the other. At once Elephant and Hippo started heaving on the rope. They heaved and they pulled for hours. The sun went down, and they heaved all night. The sun came up again, and still they heaved until they could heave no more and fell down exhausted.

They rested and when they staggered to their feet, both animals wondered just how Hare had managed it and started walking towards each other. When they met, they untied the rope from each other's waists.

"Next time we see Hare, let's kill him," they said.

The next day Hare went out and was rather pleased to see that the ground was all churned up. Just ready to plant my seeds in, he thought, and just think – I didn't even have to do any heavy digging and ploughing. Won't my wife be pleased with me!

Till Owlyglass

Till took the little donkey to the stable of the inn where he was staying and off went the professors, still giggling. They were sure they had fooled Till this time.

Now Till went to the bookbinders and bought a book with no words in it. And afterwards he went back to the inn and on each page of the book he painted some letters. And he sent for the professors again, and back they came.

"He can't have done it," said one.

"No one can teach a donkey to read," said another.

"The man's an idiot," said a third.

"Gentlemen," said Till, leading the professors into the stable. "My pupil can't read many words yet, but he's made a start. Let me show you."

Till led the donkey up to the book and slipped a few oats between the pages.

The donkey got excited and began to look for the oats, turning the pages of the book. As he turned them, he brayed, "Eee-arr, eee-arr, eee-arr."

And what Till had painted on the pages of the book were the letters E and R.

"Eee-arr, eee-arr, eee-arr!" the donkey went on.

"There," said Till. "He's a bit slow, but he's coming on, the clever little fellow, don't you think? Give me a bit more time and I'll soon have him reading fluently."

The professors did not know where to look, or what to say. So they wrapped their long gowns around themselves and hurried out of the stable. Till had certainly taught them a lesson.

* * *

© Michael Rosen (Walker Books)

SIR GALAHAD

Look at my once fertile kingdom, completely barren, and my people dying in droves. What can I do, Merlin?

Only the magical Grail has the power to cure these ills. Even the great Merlin is powerless.

As the years and adventures passed, Knights were killed or died, but always others came to fill their place. But still the Siege Perilous stood empty. The time came when Britain was devastated by famine and plague which, Merlin told the assembled Knights, only the finding of the Grail could bring to an end.

Suddenly, there was a loud banging as a gust of wind slammed shut all the palace doors.

Then, as if from nowhere, an ancient man, dressed in white, appeared in the great hall.

Then came a young knight dressed in red, without sword or shield.

As the court watched in silent wonder, the old man led the Red Knight to the Siege Perilous. There, golden letters began to appear, spelling out the young Knight's name.

SIR GALAHAD THE HIGH PRINCE

As the Knight took his seat, everyone marvelled that one so young should sit there. But King Arthur was delighted to have his Knights of the Round Table complete at last.

I know it's for you, son.

NEVER SHALL MAN TAKE ME HENCE, BUT ONLY HE BY WHOSE SIDE I OUGHT TO HANG, AND HE SHALL BE THE BEST KNIGHT IN THE WORLD.

Sir Lancelot realized with joy that Sir Galahad was his son, born to Princess Elaine. He led young Sir Galahad to the river where he had, that morning, seen a floating stone with a sword buried in it. As Lancelot had hoped, Sir Galahad withdrew the sword with ease. But still his son had no shield.

© Marcia Williams (Walker Books)

AESOP'S FABLES

THINGS ARE NOT ALWAYS WHAT THEY SEEM

There was a dog which was fond of eating eggs. Mistaking a shell-fish for an egg one day, he opened his mouth wide and bolted it with one great gulp. The weight of it in his stomach caused him intense pain. "Serve me right," he said, "for thinking that anything round must be an egg."

People who rush at things without using judgement run themselves into strange and unexpected dangers.

KNOW YOUR LIMITATIONS

A man owned a Maltese spaniel and an ass. He made a habit of playing with the dog, and whenever he dined out he used to bring back something to give it when it came and fawned on him. The ass was jealous; and one day it ran up to its master and frisked around him ~ with the result that the master received a kick which made him so angry that he told his servants to drive the ass off with blows and tie it to its manger.

Nature has not endowed us all with the same powers. There are things that some of us cannot do.

Penguin Classics

The Austere Academy

If you have walked into a museum recently – whether you did so to attend an art exhibition or to escape from the police – you may have noticed a type of painting known as a triptych. A triptych has three panels, with something different painted on each of the panels. For instance, my friend Professor Reed made a triptych for me, and he painted fire on one panel, a typewriter on another, and the face of a beautiful, intelligent woman on the third. The triptych is entitled *What Happened to Beatrice* and I cannot look upon it without weeping.

I am a writer, and not a painter, but if I were to try and paint a triptych entitled *The Baudelaire Orphans' Miserable Experiences at Prufrock Prep*, I would paint Mr Remora on one panel, Mrs Bass on another, and a box of staples on the third, and the results would make me so sad that between the Beatrice triptych and the Baudelaire triptych I would scarcely stop weeping all day.

Mr Remora was Violet's teacher, and he was so terrible that Violet thought that she'd almost rather stay in the Orphans Shack all morning and eat her meals with her hands tied behind her back rather than hurry to Room One and learn from such a wretched man. Mr Remora had a dark and thick moustache, as if somebody had chopped off a gorilla's thumb and stuck it above Mr Remora's lip, and also like a gorilla, Mr Remora was constantly eating bananas. Bananas are a fairly delicious fruit and contain a healthy amount of potassium, but after watching Mr Remora shove banana after banana into his mouth, dropping banana peels on the floor and smearing banana pulp on his chin and in his moustache, Violet never wanted to see another banana again.

Lemony Snicket

Travel

The railroad track is miles away,
    And the day is loud with voices speaking,
Yet there isn't a train goes by all day
    But I hear its whistle shrieking.

All night there isn't a train goes by,
    Though the night is still for sleeping and dreaming,
But I see its cinders red on the sky,
    And hear its engine steaming.

My heart is warm with the friends I make,
    And better friends I'll not be knowing;
Yet there isn't a train I wouldn't take,
    No matter where it's going.

Edna St Vincent Millay

An Elegy on the Death of a Mad Dog

Good people all, of every sort,
  Give ear unto my song;
And if you find it wondrous short,
  It cannot hold you long.

In Islington there was a man,
  Of whom the world might say,
That still a godly race he ran,
  Whene'er he went to pray.

A kind and gentle heart he had,
  To comfort friends and foes;
The naked every day he clad,
  When he put on his clothes.

And in that town a dog was found,
  As many dogs there be,
Both mongrel, puppy, whelp, and hound,
  And curs of low degree.

This dog and man at first were friends;
  But when a pique began,
The dog, to gain his private ends,
  Went mad, and bit the man.

Around from all the neighbouring streets
  The wondering neighbours ran,
And swore the dog had lost his wits,
  To bite so good a man.

The wound it seemed both sore and sad
  To every Christian eye;
And while they swore the dog was mad,
  They swore the man would die.

But soon a wonder came to light,
  That showed the rogues they lied;
The man recovered of the bite,
  The dog it was that died.

Oliver Goldsmith

Journey of the Magi

"A cold coming we had of it,
Just the worst time of the year
For a journey, and such a long journey:
The ways deep and the weather sharp,
The very dead of winter."
And the camels galled, sore-footed, refractory,
Lying down in the melting snow.
There were times we regretted
The summer palaces on slopes, the terraces,
And the silken girls bringing sherbet.
Then the camel men cursing and grumbling
And running away, and wanting their liquor and women,
And the night-fires going out, and the lack of shelters,
And the cities hostile and the towns unfriendly
And the villages dirty and charging high prices:
A hard time we had of it.
And the end we preferred to travel all night,
Sleeping in snatches,
With the voices singing in our ears, saying
That this was all folly.

Then at dawn we came down to a temperate valley,
Wet, below the snow line, smelling of vegetation,
With a running stream and a water-mill beating the
      darkness,
And three trees on the low sky.
And an old white horse galloped away in the meadow.
Then we came to a tavern with vine-leaves over the lintel,
Six hands at an open door dicing for pieces of silver,
And feet kicking the empty wine-skins.
But there was no information, so we continued
And arrived at evening, not a moment too soon
Finding the place; it was (you may say) satisfactory.

All this was a long time ago, I remember,
And I would do it again, but set down
This set down
This: were we led all that way for
Birth or Death? There was a Birth, certainly,
We had evidence and no doubt. I had seen birth and
      death,
But had thought they were different; this Birth was
Hard and bitter agony for us, like Death, our death.
We returned to our places, these Kingdoms,
But no longer at ease here, in the old dispensation,
With an alien people clutching their gods.
I should be glad of another death.

TS Eliot

Fairy Tale

He built himself a house,
     his foundations,
     his stones,
     his walls,
     his roof overhead,
     his chimney and smoke,
     his view from the window.

He made himself a garden,
     his fence,
     his thyme,
     his earthworm,
     his evening dew.

He cut out his bit of sky above.

And he wrapped the garden in the sky
and the house in the garden
and packed the lot in a handkerchief

and went off
lone as an arctic fox
through the cold
unending
rain
into the world.

Miroslav Holub

SIR GAWAIN

In the Middle Ages, particularly strong ties linked a man and his sister's son. This was the relationship between King Arthur and Sir Gawain, who was the son of Arthur's sister, Morgause, and King Lot of Orkney.

Medieval romances stretched Gawain's character in opposite directions. In the wonderful English poem known as *Sir Gawain and the Green Knight*, Gawain is an absolute model of bravery and courtesy, and yet what makes him especially appealing is that he is not quite perfect. He allows himself to be tempted by the beautiful wife of his host. He is a human being! Some French writers, though, show Gawain in a very different light – cheating, disloyal, bitter and violent. But on these points, everyone agrees: Gawain was one of the most important of Arthur's knights. Like the sun, he grew stronger hour by hour until noon, and then weaker hour by hour after noon; he rode a horse called Gringalet; and his terrible feud with his dearest friend, Sir Lancelot, who accidentally killed Gawain's brothers Gareth and Gaheris while saving Queen Guinevere from burning, was a mortal blow to the fellowship of the Round Table.

In 1485, the printer William Caxton listed the evidence which proved (he said) the existence of King Arthur and his fellowship: the king's tomb at Glastonbury, the Round Table at Winchester, the king's red wax seal at Westminster, Sir Lancelot's sword (he doesn't say where!) – and in Dover Castle, Sir Gawain's skull.

Kevin Crossley-Holland

The Sun

The Sun, like all stars, is a ball of fiercely **hot gas**. Hydrogen gas deep inside it is constantly being turned into helium. This releases energy in the form of **light** and **heat**.

The Sun is the nearest star to Earth. In Space terms it is relatively close – only about 150 million km away! The Sun has shone steadily for thousands of millions of years. If it went dim for only a few days, most life forms on Earth would perish.

Features of the Sun

These are some of the Sun's more **spectacular features**:

● Enormous eruptions of gas, called prominences, rise continually from the surface of the Sun. Some reach out into Space as far as 2 million km.

Arched prominences

Sunspots

● Sunspots are darker, cooler areas that appear on the Sun's surface from time to time. Some are much larger than the Earth and can last for months. Smaller ones last for only a few days or weeks.

● Every 11 years or so, sunspots become more common and then fade away. This is called the sunspot cycle.

Sun facts

● The diameter or distance through the centre of the Sun is 1,392,000km.

● The temperature at the core is believed to be about 14 million °C. At the surface it is 6000°C.

Solar flares

● Solar flares are violent explosions of energy from the Sun's surface. They shoot particles at high speed out into Space. On Earth they can produce strange effects, such as the glowing lights, called aurorae, that sometimes appear in the night sky.

Pam Beasant © Kingfisher Books

Wind scale... according to Humphrys, a good 10–12 miles' walk with a "really strong wind beating against you is the most energising and wonderful sensation". The Pembrokeshire Coast Path is a challenging hike even for hardened walkers, but offers spectacular rewards such as the view over Marloes Sands

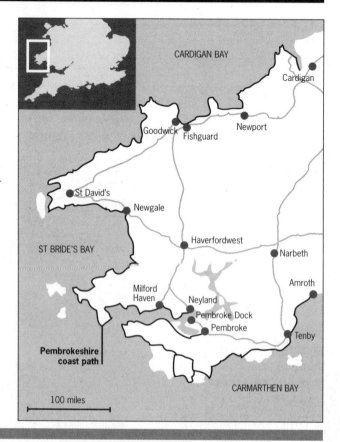

The path that's not a promenade

Anyone walking the full length of the Pembrokeshire Coast Path is certain to end up with a deep tan – from the wind, if not the sun – and calf muscles like Popeye.

The route covers 186 winding, undulating miles –100 of them on spectacular clifftops – and a total ascent and descent of 35,000ft, which is a bit like climbing Everest. The terrain is so rough that when the path was made in the 1960s, they used a small bulldozer to cut through the gorse and blackthorn that cling to the slopes. Even a hardened walker will need 10 days or more to get from Cardigan at the northern end to Amroth in the south.

It's not clear how many people do the whole thing, but about 150 a year are serious enough to register at checkpoints and get a signed certificate from the Pembrokeshire Coast National Park Authority. A recent survey showed that 300,000 people a year set foot on the path and 12,000 cover "a significant distance".

The reward is a rich diet of 500ft cliffs, crashing surf, seal-covered rocks, smugglers' coves, gleaming beaches and multiple relics of the early Celtic church. The only blots are the refineries of Milford Haven and Pembroke power station, but you can dodge these by bus.

Anthony Richards, access officer for the national park authority, says the most popular part is round the cathedral town of St David's and the westernmost tip of Wales. His nominations for best cliff, best beach and best fishing village are Stackpole Head on the southern section, Marloes Sands, and Porth-gain, between Fishguard and St David's.

"I must stress the challenging nature of this path," he says. "It's not a promenade, it's a mountain along a coast. We can give advice about the gentler sections, and there are some places accessible by wheelchair. The path is safe, but not the coast itself."

Every spring, when the coastal flowers are at their best, the authority organises a guided walk along the entire route, with naturalists, ornithologists, archaeologists and geologists. It costs £120, excluding accommodation, and this year runs from May 27 to June 9.

Guides to transport and accommodation along the path are published by the Pembrokeshire Coast National Park.Authority, Winch Lane, Haverfordwest SA61 1PY, tel 01437 764636, or visit www.pembrokeshirecoast.org.uk

The Stars

The stars in the sky look small because they are so far away. In fact they are huge. Each star is a glowing **ball of gases** held together by gravity. Most of this gas is **hydrogen**. In the hot fury of a star's 'core', or centre, hydrogen reaches a temperature of at least 10 million °C.

The heat inside a star changes hydrogen atoms into the atoms of another gas called **helium**.

When this happens there is an '**atomic reaction**' and a flash of energy is given out. Billions of these flashes of energy keep the star hot and make it shine.

The **Sun** is the nearest star to Earth. It is only a middle-sized star but it looks big to us because it is so close – only 150 million km away!

The birth and death of a star

Stars are born in clusters. A **cloud of gas and dust** called a **nebula** breaks up over millions of years into smaller clouds which are then pulled tighter and smaller by their own gravity. Eventually they heat up and start to shine.

Gravity → Core ← Gravity

A star being formed from gas and dust

- After billions of years, stars finally run out of energy and die.

Supernova

Red giant

- The remains of a very large star may collapse to form a black hole.

- Larger stars do not last as long as smaller ones. They die dramatically in an explosion. The exploding star is called a supernova.

- As a star grows old, its core becomes hotter and swells up. This swollen star is called a red giant.

Black hole

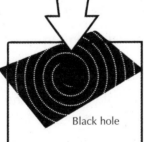
Pulsar

White dwarf

- A black hole is invisible because light cannot escape from it.

- A very small, extremely dense body is left, called a neutron star.
- Some neutron stars, called pulsars, give off pulses of light and radio waves as they spin.

- Eventually the star collapses and becomes a white dwarf – a small but very hot star. It cools and finally fades away.

Pam Beasant © Kingfisher Books

The game

Free kicks

You are awarded a free kick if you are fouled by the opposition. A free kick can be direct (from which you can score), or indirect (from which you cannot directly score). Direct free kicks are awarded for the more serious offences.

Corner kick

Your team is given a corner kick if the opposition kicks the ball over their own goal line.

Penalty kick

A penalty kick is awarded to the opposition if you commit a foul inside your own penalty area, irrespective of the position of the ball, provided it is in play. It is a shot at the goal taken from the penalty spot with only the goalkeeper to beat.

Fouls

If a player commits a foul, a free kick is awarded to the opposite team. For persistent rule-breaking, a player is cautioned and shown a yellow card. If a player is shown a yellow card twice they are sent off the field. For serious fouls a player is shown a red card and sent off immediately. In both cases the player cannot be replaced by another player.

Offside rule

The offside rule is devised to stop players loitering around the opposition's goal. You are offside if you are nearer to your opponents' goal line than the ball, when the ball touches or is played by one of your team. It is not an offence to be in an offside position unless you are interfering with play or gaining an advantage, in which case the opposite team gets a free kick. You are not offside if you receive the ball from a throw-in, goal kick, corner kick, or drop ball. You are also not offside if there are two or more opponents between you and the goal line.

Gary Lineker © Dorling Kindersley

DANGER BY MOONLIGHT

So now we stand outside the great arched gateway. It is dawn. Within the high walls, we can see the tops of the trees and clouds of green parrots swooping and screeching as they greet the new day. We hear the call to prayer. The echo reaches us; long, long, reverberations of:

Allahu-Akbar

Ash-hadu-alla-ilaha-illallah

Ash-hadu anna Muhammadar-Rasulullah

Hayya-alassalah

Hayya-alal-Falah

Allahu Akbar

La ilahu illallah

There is a sense of immense peace and goodness. The gatekeepers unroll themselves from their blankets and greet us as we enter the dark green gardens. Night still hangs in shadows and stretches long-fingered across the lawns. The great sky turns silver. Our hearts stop. The light strikes an opaque shape. It is a dome; a vast dome – bigger than any I have ever seen. More and more light pours through a crack in the dawn sky. The dome floats moon-white, like a giant lotus, and lights up the four white minarets standing like handmaidens at each corner.

Carlo hides his eyes as if he has seen a vision. "Is it really there?" he asks, awestruck.

He looks again. "Yes, yes! It is still there."

But I am silent. I remember Shah Jehan holding The Ocean of the Moon in his fingers, suspended in the candlelight so that the gems were filled with air, fire, water and ice. I seem to see it again now – but huge and overwhelming, as if we stand within the jewel itself. I too shut my eyes, expecting that such beauty cannot be real, that it will have vanished when we open them again. But it hasn't. We stare in utter silence, watching the dawn sliding pale pink over the white marble.

We have been standing for three hours. The sun is riding high in an azure sky, the dome is too white, too bright to look at, but still we stand, dazzled, speaking occasionally in hushed voices. Beyond, we see the glittering River Jamuna, and the fields stretching away to a shimmering horizon. A distant camel train picks its way through the shallows. Life goes on.

Jamila Gavin

Term 3: Novels from a variety of cultures and traditions

Black Angels

"You've had a long day, now, haven't you, Celli?"

I thought that after everything that had happened I would have been glad just to see Sophie alive, but I found myself burning up with anger toward her. "What do you think, Sophie?" I asked, all filled with spit.

"I think you did, missy, and don't use that tone with me. Just 'cause I been gone for one day don't give you the right to talk bad to me."

"You don't know what I've been through tonight, Sophie. You have no idea where I've been." Then the words ran right out of me like a river. "If you weren't involved with this stupid Movement, I wouldn't be here right now getting you out of jail. I wouldn't have been at the Screaming River Church tonight with the Klan throwing fire bottles through the windows. And I'd have a few friends left whose mothers wouldn't be afraid to invite me into their houses. If you could just keep quiet for once, Sophie, and know your place, maybe I could have a normal life".

Sophie sat up taller in her seat. "You think this is all about *you*? Is that what you think? You think because you were inconvenienced tonight, I should stop speaking the truth. You got to wake up, girl! This isn't about you. This is bigger than you. It's bigger than any of us. Can't you see that? My people have a chance to take back their power, their dignity. Nothing is more important to me than that, Celli. Nothing. Do you understand?" I nodded my head. Tears welled up in my eyes and Sophie's, too.

"I'm just tired of worrying about you, Sophie. I worry about you every day. All the time. I thought they killed you today. I thought you were never coming home. Not ever." Sophie wiped a tear from my cheek.

"We all get tired, honey," she said, folding me into her arms. "But we can't give up. Not now."

Rita Murphy

TRAVELLERS' TALES

Extract 1

The scene in the woods was tragic. The big Alsatian was lying on the ground, its paw in a cruel steel trap. Two policemen were kneeling beside the animal and one of them was stroking its head while it howled plaintively. Of Horace and the other policeman there was no sign. Reuben, Prim, Billy and Len knelt down beside the dog.

"It's one of the big-uns," said Reuben.

"This your work?" demanded the policeman brusquely.

"Poachers," muttered Reuben.

"Oh yeah?" The policeman was cynical.

"Take it or leave it – this is poachers' work. But I don't expect you to believe me. And don't do *that*!"

The dog gave an anguished howl and the policeman dropped its paw, which he'd been trying to squeeze out of the trap.

"What the—? *You* got any ideas?"

"Yes we have," said Billy. "Shall I go and get the grease, Dad?"

"OK."

He ran off.

"We've done this before," said Prim.

"I bet you have," said the other policeman bitterly. "Getting a nice fat rabbit out, were we? Or a pheasant?"

"We never—"

But Reuben interrupted her. "Ignore him, love. He doesn't know our ways. What's the dog's name?"

"Sam," said the other policeman grudgingly.

"OK, Prim – do your stuff," said Reuben quietly.

Anthony Masters

TRAVELLERS' TALES

Extract 2

She began to stroke the dog, whispering his name over and over again. "Sam – dear old Sam. Sam. You'll be all right, my dear." The dog turned and fastened its eyes on her. "You'll be all right – my dear Sam."

A few moments later Billy came leaping back with the grease.

"All right, Billy boy – go ahead."

Billy began to spread it on the Alsatian's paw, and as he did so Prim kept stroking the dog and saying, "Come on, my dearie. It's going to be all right. My dear Sam – you're going to be all right."

The dog-handler looked at her with a new respect in his eyes. "You've got on the right side of him and all."

But the other policeman remained unconvinced. "Don't let them get round you, Derek. You know they're only springing their own traps."

Len continued to spread the grease gently.

Then Reuben said, "Prim, take his paw." She did as she was told, still talking gently and now caressing Sam with her other hand. "Now pull!"

With a very swift movement she pulled. Sam gave a little whimper and his paw was out. He lay down, panting, and licking at the paw.

"Best carry him back," said Reuben. "I reckon that's broken."

"Well I'll be damned." They looked up to see that quite a crowd of bailiffs and Travellers had gathered. And one of the bailiffs was gazing at the Roberts in reluctant admiration. "I've never seen the like of that."

Anthony Masters

Anancy

Getting up to meet Tiger, Anancy greets him sweet-sweet. "Good afternoon, Bro Tiger."

"What d'you want?" Tiger says. "I'm in charge here."

"Mister King Tiger, I see you are in charge."

"I'm glad you see that. I'm glad you see you should call me Mister King Tiger."

"Position can make a man a big-big man."

"I'm doing a prize, with the gold stool. You're good at good-luck, and a bit of brain. Come. Try it."

"You know I'm not an educated man," Anancy says.

"I get on. You see that. Copy me. Hear what I say. Win the gold stool."

Anancy laughs at how clever Bro Tiger thinks he has become. He knows Tiger believes he'll count the stools and die. But Anancy doesn't say he knows Tiger thinks that. Instead, Anancy says, "You mean if I win I'll have gold and be rich. And you will be a king already. So both of us can be proud and be good friends. Do you mean that?"

"Yes. Yes." Tiger answers without thinking. Impatient, he goes on. "Come on then. Come. Count the stools. All of them in one go."

Anancy counts, "One. Two. Three. Four. Five. Six. Seven. Eight. Nine. And one more."

Tiger looks up surprised, puzzled and then gets cross. "That isn't proper counting."

"All right, Mister King Tiger. It's not a time to burn yourself out getting vex. I can try again."

"Right. But better this time. Better this time."

Anancy counts again. "One. Two. Three. Four. Five. Six. Seven. Eight. And two more."

Tiger leaps up and stamps about in a rage. "Stupid, fool-fool man. Stupid, fool-fool man. Can't count! Can't count properly!" Tiger turns round in his rage, carried away with his anger. He points to the stools, saying, "Fool-fool man, count like this, One. Two. Three. Four. Five. Six. Seven Eight. Nine. Ten." Tiger drops down, rolls over, dead, showing his belly.

THE THREE MAGI

To Lech Dymarski

They will probably come just after the New Year.

As usual, early in the morning.

The forceps of the door bell will pull you out by the head

from under the bedclothes; dazed as a newborn baby,

you'll open the door. The star of an ID

will flash before your eyes.

Three men. In one of them you'll recognise

with sheepish amazement (isn't this a small

world) your schoolmate of years ago.

Since that time he'll hardly have changed,

only grown a moustache,

perhaps gained a little weight.

They'll enter. The gold of their watches will glitter (isn't

this a grey dawn), the smoke from their cigarettes

will fill the room with a fragrance like incense.

All that's missing is myrrh, you'll think half-consciously—

while with your heel you're shoving under the couch the book they mustn't find—

what is this myrrh, anyway,

you'd have to finally look it up

someday. You'll come

with us, sir. You'll go

with them. Isn't this a white snow.

Isn't this a black Fiat.

Wasn't this a vast world.

Stanislaw Baranczak

Morning

Day came in
on an old brown bus
with two friends.
She crept down
an empty street
bending over
to sweep the thin dawn away.
With her broom,
she drew red streaks
in the corners
of the dusty sky
and finding a rooster still asleep,
prodded him into song.
A fisherman,
not far from the shore,
lifted his eyes,
saw her coming,
and yawned.
The bus rolled by,
and the two friends caught
a glimpse of blue
as day swung around a corner
to where the sea met a road.
The sky blinked,
woke up, and might have changed its mind,
but day had come.

Dionne Brand

Term 3: Poems from a variety of cultures and traditions

Tao Te Ching

What is firmly established cannot be uprooted.
What is firmly grasped cannot slip away.
It will be honoured from generation to generation.

Cultivate Virtue in yourself,
And Virtue will be real.
Cultivate it in the family,
And Virtue will abound.
Cultivate it in the village,
And Virtue will grow.
Cultivate it in the nation,
And Virtue will be abundant.
Cultivate it in the universe,
And Virtue will be everywhere.

Therefore look at the body as body;
Look at the family as family;
Look at the village as village;
Look at the nation as nation;
Look at the universe as universe.

How do I know the universe is like this?
By looking!

Lao Tzu

Translated by Gia-Fu Feng and Jane English

PICNIC POEM

In our car in our car
In our c-c-car
In our car in our car
In our wonderful car

We're up and away it's a beautiful day
Zooming along down the main highway
Dad at the wheel picnic in the boot
Sunlight and laughter planning the route.

In our car in our car
In our c-c-car
In our car in our car
In our wonderful car

Crunch bang, What's that?
Crunch bang, What's that?
A whistle and a knock, a thumping shock
A whining fizz and a crack on the block
A rattle and splutter, a groaning mutter
Cuts through the racket like a knife through butter.

That's our car that's our car
That's our wonderful car
That's our car that's our car
That's our Shhhhhhhhhhhh

Crunch bang. What's that?
Crunch bang. What's that?
A shove and a kick, dad's got a stick
And he's banging on the engine cos it makes him sick
A mallet and a crowbar, to try to make it go far
He'd be better off trying to drive my Granny's sofa

We've stopped, we're stuck, we're out of luck
Waiting for the man with the breakdown truck
Out with the picnic up with the bonnet
We'll be stuck here for hours you can bet your life upon it

In our car in our car
In our c-c-car
In our car in our car
In our useless car

David Harmer

STOPPING BY WOODS ON A SNOWY EVENING

Whose woods these are I think I know.
His house is in the village though;
He will not see me stopping here
To watch his woods fill up with snow.

My little horse must think it queer
To stop without a farmhouse near
Between the woods and frozen lake
The darkest evening of the year.

He gives his harness bells a shake
To ask if there is some mistake.
The only other sound's the sweep
Of easy wind and downy flake.

The woods are lovely, dark and deep,
But I have promises to keep,
And miles to go before I sleep,
And miles to go before I sleep.

Robert Frost

Sport on TV

Once again TV's obsession with sport destroyed our choice of viewing (Saturday 13 April). Not content with five-and-a-quarter hours on BBC1, five hours 50 minutes on ITV and two hours ten minutes on Channel 4, BBC2 then took off its tribute to Billy Wilder and replaced it with Masters golf.

It may be a surprise to those making this decision, but there are licence-payers out here who have no interest in sport and feel entitled to an alternative.

I also object to the changing of published schedules, except when made necessary by vital breaking news or the need to meet other demands of national significance. Golf does not fall into those categories.

I dread this summer, with the usual Wimbledon, athletics and cricket being joined by World Cup soccer. Will there be anything for me to watch?

Jeffrey Butcher

Waltham Abbey, Essex

The BBC apologised for changing the schedule, but because rain had stopped play on the Friday, the second round had to be completed earlier the following day. As the BBC has the live rights to this coverage, it was obliged to broadcast the competition. Sunset Boulevard will be shown on 11 May.

Radio Times

Age of majority is not a minor matter

YOUR article on giving 16-year-olds the vote (*TES*, April 12) highlighted what we, the Liberal Democrat Youth and Students, are committed to.

We believe that this campaign is important because there are many injustices in the current British democracy. At present, 16-year-olds can get a full-time job and pay taxes, join the armed services, marry, and even have a family, yet they have no say over which government forms the policies which affect them and other issues important to them. For example, they are forced to accept a government that will introduce tuition fees and have no influence on how the education policy for their children will develop.

Sixteen-year-olds are both mature enough to vote and interested in helping to decide their government. Voter apathy among the young stems not from disinterest but from a belief that their views are being ignored.

While it might be argued that young people are insufficiently educated to vote we would point to the forthcoming introduction of citizenship teaching in schools.

Young people will be educated about how to vote and about other aspects of politics but then, once you have built up that knowledge and enthusiasm, there will be a two-year gap, until they reach 18, to put it into practice, which makes a farce of the situation.

Miranda Piercy
Chair, Liberal Democrat Youth and Students
4 Cowley Street
Westminster, London SW1

edleader

As part of its attempt to improve behaviour in schools, curb truancy and cut crime, the Government has announced that headteachers facing the toughest behavioural challenges – those in some inner city schools – will be offered the chance to have a police officer stationed in or around the school. Many people will be asking themselves how and why society has stooped so low that we need police patrols to maintain order in our schools and to ensure that pupils remain inside (and intruders remain outside) the perimeters of the school fence. But if the programme unfolds as the Government intends, it will not only provide valuable back-up for teachers, it should bring enormous benefits in terms of breaking down barriers, changing children's attitudes towards authority and building a sense of community in our inner cities. Pilot initiatives in London are certainly a testament to this. Early figures from a pilot scheme in Southwark schools suggest that a police presence may have reduced truancy-related crime in the area by as much as 95 per cent.

Dictionary definitions

❶

cult (*say* kult) *noun*
1 a religion **2** a thing or person that is popular only with a small group of people: *a cult film*

cultivate (*say* **kul**-ti-vate) *verb*
1 to prepare and work land in order to plant and raise crops **2** to make something stronger and better: *to cultivate friendships*

Word Family: cultivation *noun*
Similar Meaning: for definition 1 **till**

cultivated (*say* **kul**-ti-vay-ted) *adjective*
1 produced by or using cultivation: *cultivated land* **2** well-educated and well-behaved

culture (*say* **kul**-cher) *noun*
1 the ideas, knowledge and beliefs of a particular society or group of people: *Aboriginal culture* **2** art, literature, music and so on

❷

cult *kult, n.* **1** a system of religious belief. **2** a sect. **3** great devotion to: *the cult of physical fitness.*
[Same root as **cultivate**.]
cultivate *kul'ti-vāt, v.t.* **1** to till or prepare (ground) for crops. **2** to grow (a crop). **3** to develop, or improve, by care or study: *to cultivate good manners.* **4** to encourage (e.g. science, friendship). **5** to seek the company of (a person).
cultivā'tion *n.* **1** the art or practice of cultivating. **2** a refined, cultivated state.
cul'tivator *n.* an implement for breaking up ground, esp. among crops.
culture *kul'chủr, n.* **1** cultivation. **2** educated refinement. **3** a type of civilisation: *Bronze Age culture.*
cul'tural *adj.* **cul'turally** *adv.*
cul'tured *adj.* **1** cultivated. **2** well educated, refined.
[L. *colĕre, cultum,* to till, worship.]

❸

Cult, kult, *n.* a system of religious belief, worship. — also **Cult'us.** [L. *cultus—colĕre,* to worship.]
Culter, kul'tėr, *n.* obsolete form of **Coulter.** —*adjs.* **Cultiros'tral, Culturos'tral; Cul'trate, -d,** shaped like a pruning-knife; **Cul'triform,** in the form of a pruning-knife: sharp-edged.
Cultism, kult'ism, *n.* a style of writing after the manner of Luis de Góngora y Argote (1561–1627), a Spanish lyric poet—*estilo culto,* being florid, pedantic, often obscure (see **Gongorism**). —*ns.* **Cult'ist, Cult'erist.** [Sp. *culte,* elegant—L. *cultus.*]
Cultivate, kul'ti-vāt, *v.t.* to till or produce by tillage: to prepare for crops: to devote attention to: to civilise or refine.—*adjs.* **Cul'tivable, Cultivat'able,** capable of being cultivated.—*ns.* **Cultivā'tion,** the art or practice of cultivating: civilisation: refinement; **Cul'tivator.**— **Cultivate** a person's friendship, to endeavour to get his good-will. [Low L. *cultivāre, -ātum—*L. *colĕre,* to till, to worship.]
Culture, kul'tūr, *n.* cultivation: the state of being cultivated: refinement the result of cultivation.—*v.t.* to cultivate: to improve.—*adjs.* **Cul'turable; Cul'tural.**—*p. adj.* **Cul'tured,** cultivated: well educated: refined.—*adj.* **Cul'tureless.** [L. *cultūra—colĕre.*]
Cultus. See **Cult.**

Thesaurus entries

❶

say *verb*
1 *Colin tried to say what he really thought.* ▶ to state, to express, to convey, to explain
2 *I said that it was getting late.* ▶ to mention, to remark, to comment
3 *She was too angry to say his name.* ▶ to speak, to utter

saying *noun*
There is a saying that an apple a day keeps the doctor away. ▶ a proverb, an adage, a maxim, a motto, a slogan

scale *verb*
The climbers began to scale the rock face. ▶ to climb, to ascend, to mount

scales *plural noun*
The cat was too heavy to weigh in the scales. ▶ a balance

scamper *verb*
You could hear the mice scampering back into their holes. ▶ to scurry, to scuttle, to dash, to hurry, to run

scan *verb*
1 *We scanned the landscape for signs of a road.* ▶ to study, to survey, to view, to gaze at, to scrutinize, to examine
2 *She scanned the book for a picture of the village.* ▶ to look through, to glance through, to skim, to read quickly

scandal *noun*
1 *Their behaviour caused quite a scandal.* ▶ a sensation, an outrage, an embarrassment
2 *The newspaper article was full of scandal.* ▶ gossip, rumour

scandalous *adjective*
Their behaviour had not just been embarrassing but downright scandalous. ▶ disgraceful, outrageous, shameful, shocking

scanty *adjective*
The furniture in the house was old and scanty. ▶ sparse, meagre, inadequate

scar *noun*
The man had a scar on his left cheek. ▶ a mark, a blemish

scar *verb*
His face had been scarred in an accident. ▶ to mark, to disfigure, to damage

scarce *adjective*
Fresh fruit was scarce because of the war. ▶ short, in short supply, lacking, sparse, meagre, limited, scanty

scarcely *adverb*
Donna had scarcely finished eating when the phone rang. ▶ barely, hardly, only just

scare *verb*
The noise was scaring the animals. ▶ to frighten, to alarm, to startle, to terrify

scare *noun*
You gave me quite a scare. ▶ a fright, a shock

scary *adjective*
(informal) *It was scary in the dark.* ▶ creepy, eerie, frightening, ghostly, spooky, uncanny, weird

| ❷ | **say** | *v* | tell, state, declare, speak, express |
| | **scarce** | *adj* | rare, short, few, uncommon |

❶ The Oxford Children's Thesaurus ❷ Better Words: A First Thesaurus

Acknowledgements

The publishers gratefully acknowledge permission to reproduce the following copyright material:

Ashgate Publishing Ltd for *Tao Te Ching* by Lao Tsu, translated by Gia-Fu Feng and Jane English © 1972, Gia-Fu Feng and Jane English (1972, Wildwood House). **Atlantic Syndication** for the news story 'Unhappy ending for the newborn hippo rescued from a lake' from the *Daily Mail*, 4th June, 1998 © 1998, Daily Mail. **Stanislaw Baranczak** for 'The Three Magi' from *Spoiling Cannibals for Fun: Polish Poetry of the Last Two Decades of Communist Rule* by Stanislaw Baranczak, edited and translated by Stanislaw Baranczak and Clare Cavanagh © 1991, Stanislaw Baranczak (1991, Northwestern University Press). **Elizabeth Barnett, Literary Executor, New York,** for 'Travel' by Edna St Vincent Millay from *Collected Poems* ©1921, 1934, 1948 & 1962, Edna St Vincent Millay (1962, HarperCollins). **Bloomsbury Publishing** for 'No-Speaks' from *The Frog Who Dreamed she was an Opera Singer* by Jackie Kay © 1998, Jackie Kay (1998, Bloomsbury). **Dionne Brand** for 'Morning' from *Earth Magic* by Dionne Brand © 1998, Dionne Brand (1998, Sister Vision Press, Toronto). **Jeffrey Butcher** for a letter to the *Radio Times* (27 April to 3 May 2002) © 2002, Jeffrey Butcher (2002, BBC Publications). **Chambers Harrap Publishers Ltd** for an extract from *Chambers Handy Dictionary* © 1993, Chambers Harrap, and an extract from *Chambers Twentieth Century Dictionary* © 1901, WR Chambers Ltd. **The Controller of HMSO** for extracts from the National Literacy Strategy: *Framework for Teaching* © Crown copyright 1998. **Curtis Brown Literary Agents** for an extract from *Death by Spaghetti: Bizarre, baffling and bonkers* by Paul Sussman © 1996, Paul Sussman (1996, Fourth Estate Ltd). **Egmont Children's Books** for an extract from *A Series of Unfortunate Events: The Austere Academy* by Lemony Snicket © 2000, Lemony Snicket (2000, HarperCollins, USA; 2002, Egmont Children's Books, UK). **Faber & Faber Ltd** for an extract from 'Journey of the Magi' from *Collected Poems 1909–1962* by TS Eliot © 1954, TS Eliot (1954, Faber & Faber Ltd). **Samuel French Ltd** on behalf of the Estate of JM Barrie for an extract from *Dear Brutus* by JM Barrie © 1931, JM Barrie (1931, Hodder & Stoughton). **Katherine Froman** for the poem 'Homeweb' from *Seeing Things* by Robert Froman © 1977, Robert Froman (1977, Abelard-Schuman Ltd). **Katherine Froman** for the poem 'Sky Day Dream' from *Seeing Things* by Robert Froman © 1977, Robert Froman (1977, Abelard-Schuman Ltd). **Ginn** (part of Harcourt Education) for an extract from *The Ginn School Dictionary* by George Hunt © 1995, George Hunt (1995, Rigby Heinemann.) **The Guardian** for the article and illustration 'The path that's not a promenade' from *The Guardian*, 12 February 2000 © 2000, The Guardian (2000, The Guardian Newspapers Ltd). **The Rod Hall Agency and Philip Ridley** for an extract from the revised playscript of *Krindlekrax* by Philip Ridley © 2002, Philip Ridley (2002, Faber & Faber Ltd). **David Harmer** for the 'Picnic Poem' by David Harmer from *Creaking Down the Corridor* by David Harmer and Paul Cookson © David Harmer (BBC Verse Universe). **Her Majesty's Stationery Office** for an extract from 'Don't be a reject!' by the DVLA © 1999, Crown Copyright (1999, DETR). **David Higham Associates** for an extract from *Danger by Moonlight* by Jamila Gavin © 2002, Jamila Gavin (2002, Egmont Children's Books). **David Higham Associates** for an extract from *Step by Wicked Step* by Anne Fine © 1995, Anne Fine (1995, Hamish Hamilton). **Hodder & Stoughton Ltd** for an extract from *The Snatchers* by Helen Creswell © 1998, Helen Creswell (1998 Hodder Children's Books). **Kingfisher Publications plc** for an extract 'The Stars' from *1001 Facts About Space* by Pam Beasant © 1993, Kingfisher Publications plc (1993, Kingfisher), and an extract from 'The Sun' from *1001 Facts About Space* by Pam Beasant © 1993, Kingfisher Publications plc (1993, Kingfisher). **Liberal Democrat Youth and Students** for a letter 'Age of majority is not a minor matter' by Miranda Piercy published in *The Times Educational Supplement*, 3 May 2000 © 2002, Liberal Democrat Youth and Students (2002, News International). **Macmillan Children's Books** for an extract from *Black Angels* by Rita Murphy © 2001, Rita Murphy (2001, Macmillan Children's Books). **News Team International** for a photograph to accompany 'Unhappy ending for the newborn hippo rescued from a lake' from the *Daily Mail*, 4th June 1998 © 1998, News Team International. **Orion Children's Books** for an extract from 'Sir Gawain' from *The King who Was and Will Be* by Kevin Crossley-Holland, illustrated by Peter Malone © 1998, Kevin Crossley-Holland (1998, Orion Children's Books). **Orion Children's Books** for an extract from 'The Hunting of Death' from *Golden Myths and Legends of the World* by Geraldine McCaughrean © 1999, Geraldine McCaughrean (1999, Orion Children's Books). **Oxford University Press** for an extract 'Talk About Short' from *Short! A Book of Very Short Stories* by Kevin Crossley-Holland © 1998, Kevin Crossley-Holland (1998, Oxford University Press), and an extract from *The Oxford Children's Thesaurus* © 2000, Oxford University Press (2000, Oxford University Press). **The Penguin Group** for two extracts from *Travellers' Tales* by Anthony Masters © 1990, Anthony Masters (1990, Blackie); for 'Things are not always what they seem' from *Fables of Aesop* translated by SA Handford © 1954, SA Handford (1973, Penguin); for an extract 'Fairy Tale' from *Miroslav Holub: Selected Poems* translated by Ian Milner and George Theiner © 1967, Miroslav Holub, translation © 1967, Penguin Books (1967, Penguin Books); for 'Know your limitations' from *Fables of Aesop* translated by SA Handford © 1954, SA Handford (1973, Penguin); for an extract from *Superguides: Football* by Gary Lineker (first published as *The Young Soccer Player* © 1994, 2000 Dorling Kindersley Ltd (1994, 2000, Dorling Kindersley Ltd). **Penguin Books Australia Ltd** for an extract from *The Gizmo* by Paul Jennings © 1994, Paul Jennings (1994, Penguin Books Australia Ltd), and for an extract 'A Little Bit From the Author' from *Uncovered! Weird Weird Stories* by Paul Jennings © 1995, Paul Jennings (1995, Penguin Books Australia Ltd). **The Peters Fraser & Dunlop Group** for an extract 'Anancy counts the magic stools' from *Anancy-Spiderman* by James Berry © 1988, James Berry (1988, Walker Books Ltd), and for 'The New Poem' from *Sky in the Pie* by Roger McGough © 1983, Roger McGough (1983, Kestrel). **The Random House Group** for an extract from *The Lottie Project* by Jacqueline Wilson © 1997, Jacqueline Wilson (1997, Doubleday); for two extracts from *Krindlekrax* by Philip Ridley © 1991, Philip Ridley (1991, Jonathan Cape); for the Estate of Robert Frost and Jonathan Cape for 'Stopping by Woods on a Snowy Evening' by Robert Frost from *The Poetry of Robert Frost* edited by Edward Connery Lathem © 1951, Robert Frost (1951, Jonathan Cape). **Schofield & Sims Ltd** for an extract from *Better Words: A First Thesaurus* © 1985, Schofield & Sims Ltd (1985, Schofield & Sims Ltd) **Scholastic Ltd** for 'edleader' by Tracy Lomas, *Junior Education*, June 2002 © 2002, Scholastic Ltd (2002, Scholastic Ltd). **Walker Books Ltd** for an extract from *Till Owlyglass and the Donkey Reader* by Michael Rosen © 1990, Michael Rosen (1990, Walker Books Ltd); for an illustration and extract from 'Sir Galahad' from *King Arthur and the Knights of the Round Table* by Marcia Williams © 1996, Marcia Williams (1996, Walker Books Ltd); for 'The Tug of War' from *The Oxfam Book of Children's Stories: South and North, East and West* edited by Michael Rosen © 1992, Michael Rosen (1992, Walker Books Ltd); for extracts and illustration from *Alan Snow's Whacky Guide to Tricks and Illusions* by Louise Cook and Alan Snow © text, 1992 Louise Cook; illustration, © 1992, Alan Snow (1992, Walker Books Ltd). **The Watts Publishing Group Ltd** for an extract from 'Orpheus and Eurydice' from *The Orchard Book of Greek Myths* by Geraldine McCaughrean © 1992, Geraldine McCaughrean (1992, Orchard Books), and for 'The Creation' from *Myths and Civilisations: Ancient Egypt* by Sarah Quie © 1998, Sarah Quie (1998, Franklin Watts).

Every effort has been made to trace copyright holders for the works reproduced in this book, and the publishers apologise for any inadvertent omissions.